A Roof Over My Head

Also by Michael Green

THE ART OF COARSE RUGBY

THE ART OF COARSE SAILING

EVEN COARSER RUGBY

THE MICHAEL GREEN BOOK OF COARSE SPORT

THE ART OF COARSE GOLF

THE ART OF COARSE ACTING

DON'T PRINT MY NAME UPSIDE DOWN
(a novel)

MICHAEL GREEN

A ROOF OVER MY HEAD

or

The Art of Coarse Moving

HUTCHINSON OF LONDON

HUTCHINSON & CO (*Publishers*) LTD
178–202 Great Portland Street, London W1

London Melbourne Sydney
Auckland Bombay Toronto
Johannesburg New York

First published 1969

*This book has been set in Baskerville, printed in Great Britain
on Antique Wove paper by Anchor Press, and
bound by Wm. Brendon, both of Tiptree, Essex*

09 100280 x

For Richard Simon
and also
Bill, Alan and all who have suffered

Author's note

I should like to thank my old friend and solicitor (who for professional reasons must remain anonymous) for his help and advice with this book. Without him I would have finished it in half the time.

Michael Green

One

January 1 I am writing this because I received six diaries for Christmas. Sheila, my wife, gave me one, Gaye, our daughter, gave me another and Maureen, my secretary at work, gave me a third. I also received two very large ones from my old friend Jack Askew, but unfortunately they are part of a dozen which a Swedish firm sent him and he is trying to get rid of them as all the days and months are in Swedish. So is the postal information. It is not much use knowing how much it costs to send a parcel from Stockholm to Uppsala.

My old Uncle Walter has also given me a diary but it is last year's. He says I can easily alter the dates and it is a pity to waste it.

Sheila says I should keep a diary as it will be interesting to look back on in future years. The only trouble is finding material to put in it. We live such ordinary lives. Our daughter, Gaye, says it would do me good to write down my secret sexual thoughts every day. Typical of the younger generation.

January 2 I cannot think what made me write that there would be nothing to put into my diary. Just after Christmas some Australian boys moved into the flat upstairs. Last night they kept us awake until 3 a.m. having a party, although it sounded more like a West Country shin-kicking contest. I am convinced some of the guests were wearing football boots. Fell into a broken slumber only to be woken at five by the guests *going home*. We really must think about leaving this flat and getting a place of our own. I have been meaning to do so for fifteen years.

January 4 Have decided not to keep my diary every day as I get a headache trying to think of things to put in it. Sheila says she hopes I won't abandon it as it will be nice to look back at the end of the year and see what happened.

January 6 This evening a group of young girls carrying cans of beer knocked at our door and asked for the Australian boys. I am not a malicious man, but I directed them to a block of flats five streets away. As it happened I need not have bothered because the boys were not in and stayed out all night. I know, because I lay awake for hours waiting for the noise of their coming in.

January 7 No noise from upstairs this evening. What can be wrong? It is like waiting for a bomb to go off.

January 8 Our daughter, Gaye, went back to University today after borrowing ten pounds from me. She says she is going back early so she can get some extra work done. A likely tale.

January 9 I now discover that Sheila also lent Gaye ten pounds before she went back. As a result, Sheila has now borrowed ten pounds from me. Women have no sense of morals in money matters.

January 10 Sir Phillip, the managing director of our firm, came into my office today. My job is editing our monthly house magazine *The Condenser* (we are an engineering firm) and he likes to poke around occasionally and make sure his name is being mentioned frequently.

Unfortunately he asked for a proof which I could not find because the order of my folders had been disturbed. I lost my temper and said, 'Some idiot has been mucking these folders about.' He gave me an odd look and said, 'It was me. I was looking through them.' I thought of several things to say but decided to keep quiet.

As if that was not bad enough, when I got home I found the landing light had gone again and I hurt my ankle on the stairs. We really shall have to consider leaving the flats as a matter of urgency.

January 13 Landing light still not repaired. Mrs. Goldsmith downstairs complained about Sheila using the electric hair-dryer during 'Coronation Street'.

January 14 I spoke about the staircase light to Harry, the porter (although why they call him that I don't know, as he has never ported anything in his life. He just has a free flat from the owners and grumbles all day). Harry said it was not worth repairing because of the bad treatment it got from the tenants. What we pay our rent for I don't know.

January 18 I really shall not stay in this flat any longer. This evening while I was watching the television a strange stain started to spread all over the ceiling. It was like *Tess of the D'Urbervilles,* when the blood comes through from upstairs where the body is.

Then suddenly a great chunk of plaster fell off and burst like a bomb all over the floor. I rushed upstairs to the Australian boys' flat and demanded to know what was going on. They took me inside and showed me a dustbin full of home-made beer which they had upset on the living-room floor. Since they have never put down a carpet, only old copies of the *Sydney Sun,* it went straight through the floorboards to our ceiling.

They seemed unable to comprehend the seriousness of what they had done, and offered me some of the beer, which tasted awful. It took Sheila and I half an hour to clean up the mess downstairs. By the time it was finished I had a vile

Burst like a bomb all over the floor

headache. I believe I am straining my eyes writing this ridiculous diary. I shall now finish it for ever.

January 26 Decided to write diary again. It is becoming compulsive. Sheila says I should make up my mind about leaving the flat and do something instead of raging impotently. A typical woman's remark. Their mental processes are so much less complicated that they rarely suffer from indecision. It is like expecting a snail to be indecisive.

February 1 Mind still not made up.

February 3 Today the girl at the office had all the folders in the correct order. Gaye wrote to us from college and we received fifteen shillings from the football pools. In the evening Sheila and I walked over to The Crown where we met our old friend Jack Askew and his wife.

Jack has bought some new golf clubs and will give me his old putter, since I am convinced that mine is bent. I said to Sheila as we were walking back that it is really a nice district and it would be a shame to uproot ourselves, especially as we are so well settled in the flat.

February 7 At last my mind is made up. I shall not stay in this flat a moment longer. I had written to the agents asking them to repair the ceiling and today I received a reply which said that tenants were responsible for the interior decoration. In addition, when the lease runs out in a few months, the rent is to be increased by two pounds a week.

Their letter also said: 'We would take the opportunity of drawing your attention to the fact that tenants are not allowed to play ball games in the gardens, as stated in the lease. We regret the necessity for having to issue this warning.'

This is a reference to the fact that I sometimes practise golf shots on the lawn. I expect that evil old hag Mrs. Bagworth has complained because I sent a ball through her window.

She said, 'Why did you do that?' and I said, 'Because I am

bending the left elbow at the top of the backswing.' For some reason she became quite abusive.

February 8 Wrote a strong letter of protest, addressed personally to the managing director of the property company, and commencing 'Dear Scrooge'. But after posting it I recalled I had forgotten to address the envelope. As I was returning from the pillar-box I met one of the Australian lads on the stairs and he told me that their rent is to be increased as well.

I said hopefully, 'I expect you'll want to move somewhere cheaper,' and he said, no, they would get another to share (making nine in all). They have in mind someone who plays the drums in a pop group. This is the last straw.

February 12 Letter to the property owners returned today marked 'insufficiently addressed'. Placed it in a new envelope and carefully addressed it this time.

February 13 This morning I remembered I had not stamped the envelope to the property people. In the evening Sheila and I strolled round looking at houses for sale. There seems a big selection, and judging by the adverts in the papers the building societies are desperate to lend money.

February 17 Received following letter from property company:

> Dear Sir,
>
> With reference to your unstamped addressed to Mr. Scrooge, we presume the contents to mean that you will not be renewing your lease.

I wrote back to say that they could take it like that if they wished, as I intended to buy a house and be free of people like them. Buying is obviously so much more economical than renting that I cannot think why I have wasted twenty years paying rent.

As a final insult, I enclosed a stamp for their postage

adding that I did so because they were obviously in a bad way financially.

February 25 I believe the steward at the golf club is fiddling. Jack Askew and I pooled our resources into a syndicate on the fruit machine and after 15 minutes we won the jackpot. Only five sixpences came out. We pointed this out to the steward who said someone else had already won that morning. This, however, does not account for the fact that fewer sixpences came out than we put in. Askew says he will raise it with the committee. The man is obviously up to no good.

What with one thing and another I had too many Worthingtons and was late for lunch. Sheila was very distant. I can never understand why women turn Sunday lunch into a religious festival. In the afternoon I fell into an uneasy slumber when I was suddenly awakened by what I took to be a bomb exploding in a corrugated-iron factory. I then realised the noise was caused by someone playing the drums upstairs.

Since sleep was impossible I comforted myself by reading the property ads. in the papers. I really cannot stay here any longer.

February 26 When I got home tonight Sheila said, 'Well, have you done anything about moving?' I pointed out that I had a living to earn as editor of *The Condenser* and did not have all day free to wander around estate agents. Women are never happy unless they have something to grumble at.

March 1 Secured mid-day editions of evening papers at the office and studied the property advertisements. One immediately caught my eye, a small detached house in Acton, at a very reasonable price. Seized by a fit of decision, I picked up the 'phone and rang the number given in the paper. But while the number was ringing Sir Phillip came into my office and as he spoke a woman's voice answered the 'phone.

I did not want to reveal I was using the office 'phone for

private calls, which is strictly forbidden, so I said, 'Very well, old man, but this time get it done,' and hung up, trying to look as if I had just been having a business argument.

As soon as Sir Phillip had gone I rang the number again, but the woman said, 'If you are the person who has just rung up and talked a lot of gibberish I don't think we can do business.' She then hung up.

It is extremely annoying to lose the chance of a house simply because of that stupid interruption by Sir Phillip. I am sure it would have been just the place for us.

Considered telephoning again in a disguised voice, but decided against it.

When I told Sheila what had happened, she said at this rate we shall be in the flat for the rest of our lives. Women are too pessimistic. They lack the positive attitude of the male.

March 3 Electric light on stairs still not repaired.

March 4 Fourteen empty beer bottles appeared outside our flat door today. There was a note: 'Please do not put bottles in dustbin.—Porter.' This is absurd. Only one of the bottles is mine.

March 5 It is useless to buy a house from advertisements in newspapers. My ear is sore with being pressed against the telephone. Every number I ring is engaged. If I do get through I am frequently abused by the vendors.

However, about nine o'clock this evening I spoke to a man who said he would be delighted if we called round, but we should have to be quick as a lot of people were after the house. Unfortunately, it is in Uxbridge, but we have to make a start somewhere. Sheila and I will go down tomorrow.

March 6 Went straight to Uxbridge from Town and met Sheila at the station. I never realised the Piccadilly Line was so long. No one could tell us where the road we wanted was so we took a taxi.

The house looked a bargain. It had a lovely garden with goldfish pond. It seemed incredible that it was only £6,000.

I rang the bell and a man came to the door and I said I had come about the house.

He replied: 'What about the house?'

I said about buying it and he said it was not for sale. It turned out that the taxi had taken us to Lupin Gardens, not Lupin Road. Lupin Road was only five minutes' walk away but the houses were nothing like as good as in the Gardens.

After checking that the address was correct we entered the garden. Unfortunately the gate was sagging on its hinges and when I tried to force it open they gave way and it fell to the ground. Sheila said, 'Repairing the gate can be your first job when we have bought the house.'

Our feelings can be imagined when the owner told us he had sold the property only ten minutes before. However he asked us if we would like to make a provisional offer, so I named a sum well below the asking price. He became angry and asked if we thought he was giving the place away.

I pointed out that the property was not in first-class condition as the gate had fallen off its hinges when I opened it. I have never seen a person flare up so quickly. He ran down the path shouting, 'You clumsy bastard, look what you've done.' He was so rude we left without saying another word.

We had to walk back to the station. I told Sheila I felt more exhausted after looking at one house than after producing the special Christmas number of *The Condenser*.

March 8 Saw three houses this evening. One was owned by a Chinaman who did not speak English so we could not negotiate. Another smelt so bad we didn't go inside. The third was a nice house but on going inside we found that all light was blocked by a vast gasholder at the back.

The man said: 'It's all right, it goes down at weekends and the view is lovely. One thing about living near the gasworks, the smell prevents bronchitis.'

Two

March 9 The bitter at The Crown is off. Last night I was served with a cloudy glass of beer which the landlord refused to change, saying it was merely bubbles and would settle. Awoke this morning with the sort of head you get after a night's debauchery. I have not felt like this since grandmother died, but that is too long a story to go into now.

Saw good house in Ruislip advertised in evening paper but their 'phone was engaged all night. I believe they left it off the hook.

March 11 Went into The Crown again this evening, and four other people complained of stomach trouble. The landlord says there is nothing wrong with his beer, only the people that drink it.

March 18 We have decided to go to an estate agent. I cannot spend any more time marching round West London on the trail of houses which have either been sold, or are not worth buying. Also, the need for leaving the flat is becoming imperative.

The Australian lads made so much noise last night that I shouted up for them to be quiet. A few minutes later the person in the flat below came up and asked me to stop shouting and stamping around.

We have avoided estate agents so far because I believe they always blackmail the buyer into paying more than a house is worth. But unless we do something we shall have to stay in this flat for ever.

March 21 Uncle Walter called over from Harrow to see us. He cannot understand the trouble we are having.

'When your aunt and I got married, my boy,' he said, 'we got a lovely little place in Shepherd's Bush for £200, and they were glad to have the money.'

He does not understand that the Tube no longer finishes at Shepherd's Bush.

March 26 As I was going on the bus to the station this morning I saw a nice house with a For Sale notice in the garden, so I made up my mind to call this evening. On the way back home I jumped off the bus in the rain at the traffic lights, only to find SOLD pasted across the original notice. Had to walk half a mile home in the rain.

March 30 As it was Saturday we made the rounds of the local estate agents. At the first I asked for details of property up to £5,000. The man behind the desk smirked and asked if I wanted to live in London or on Cape Wrath? I didn't really think it was all that funny. Eventually I agreed to consider houses up to £7,000 and he gave me a list all of which were around £9,000.

We then went to another agent who gave us a list but more than half the houses were also on the first agent's list. By the end of the morning we had collected about half a pound of papers and went home to study them.

March 31 We are dazed with looking at bits of paper. The agents' descriptions of property are useless since all houses are described in glowing terms and their defects concealed by such jargon as 'needs slight renovation'. Askew came round to help us in the afternoon and told us a ghastly experience that happened to him.

Some years previously he had tried to sell his house and

buy another through an estate agent. The agent's description of Askew's home was so warped that Askew found himself trying to buy his own house.

April 1 We have selected the first house to visit. It is described as 'Early inspection recommended' which Askew says means 'For heaven's sake come and look at it, we can't sell the damn place.' Sheila has made an appointment.

April 2 Believe may be going insane. This evening we called at the house. We were greeted by a superior-looking woman with a husband who shuffled around in carpet slippers. The house really was in good condition and a great deal had obviously been spent on it.

There was concealed lighting in the side of the bath, and even a device for warming the lavatory seat, and a light which went on to show it was down. I could have played with it for hours if Sheila hadn't pulled me away.

Sheila and I were so pleased that I named the full asking price of £6,000. The effect on the woman was alarming. She got up from her chair and shouted, 'What did you say?' Thinking she might be hard of hearing I repeated with great emphasis, 'Six thousand pounds.'

To my surprise she screamed 'The cheek of it!' and marching to the front door, held it open for us to leave.

She almost pushed us out of the house, and slammed the door with a bang that could have been heard all over the district, and probably was, judging by the number of windows that were opened. Feeling there had been a misunderstanding I bent down and shouted through the letter-box, 'If you like I will raise the offer by fifty pounds!'

Her only reply was to charge down the hall with a broomstick and attempt to poke out my eye. As we left she shouted, 'Don't give me any more of your cheek!' It is all very baffling.

April 3 The mystery is solved. Returned to the estate agents to tell them what had happened and was greeted with the usual total indifference. Whenever I call the wretched man is always on the 'phone, engaged in some double-dealing or other.

Sincc he kept me waiting twenty minutes I could hardly avoid hearing what he said, remarks like, 'Between you and me the vendor is an old idiot and I think you could get her to reduce the price.' I have no doubt he will be telling the vendor that the buyer is a young fool who will pay the earth.

When he had finished I told my story and he discovered there was a misprint on the list. The price of the house should have been £9,000. The agent offered no apology. I suppose he needn't worry as long as he can make £10,000 a year sitting on his chair and handing out misinformation.

April 6 Wrote to the *Daily Telegraph,* demanding that estate agents should be registered and liable to long terms of imprisonment for false descriptions of property. I have not written to the papers since the MCC dropped Trevor Bailey years ago.

April 8 Amid all the calamities, I forgot to mention that our daughter Gaye has arrived home from University for the Easter holidays. She came yesterday, ate a large meal, and announced her intention of going to stay with some friends in Norfolk for a fortnight. Sheila feels rather hurt but my principal emotion is one of pity for the inhabitants of Norfolk.

April 10 Letter not published in *Daily Telegraph* yet. Sheila borrowed five pounds from me to make up for five she lent Gaye, who has not paid the ten she borrowed in the New Year.

April 12 Letter still not published in *Daily Telegraph.* We have selected another house, this time from the list of Grubshaw, Scrachitt and Thrower. It is a large old house but the price of modern property is prohibitive. It is described as 'an older-type of property ideal either as a home or for investment'. Askew said it meant you could make a small fortune by cramming it with Irish navvies until the local authority found out.

Before going to bed I amused myself by thinking how an estate agent would describe a hole in the ground: 'A pleasant, well-dug cavity, situate a few minutes' walk from Central Line station, and convenient for shops and buses. The lower part is of good London clay, exposed by the former owner at considerable expense, and the upper part is mainly loam, with a few well-chosen stones. . . .'

April 13 Obvious that the *Daily Telegraph* are not going to publish my letter. I presented myself at Grubshaw's at ten o'clock (it being Saturday) and was met by a fawning young assistant whom I nicknamed Soapy. He kept referring to Sheila as my 'lady-wife'. We drove to the house in my car and he asked me to stop in a shabby road at the back of the Marquis of Granby.

I asked him if he was lost and he said no, we were here. I could see no sign of the house so I asked where it was. He indicated a dense mass of undergrowth spilling over the pavement. The house was concealed behind this and a privet hedge now 9 ft. tall. We had some difficulty finding the gate and then had literally to hack our way to the front door, which was defended by 49 empty milk bottles.

'As you will see, sir,' said young Soapy, 'there is a lovely mature garden, although a little lacking in attention at present.'

I would have replied but at that moment a huge tomcat leaped from the bushes and started to sharpen its claws on my trousers. After beating it off we entered.

The house smelled as if someone had died there a long time ago. The wallpaper was covered in green buboes, there was damp everywhere and festoons of prehistoric electric wiring were draped from the walls. It reminded me of a wartime Army billet.

'The property is cheap because it is an executor's sale,' explained young Soapy. 'The previous owner was an old gentleman who died.'

Feeling that a joke might enliven the chilly atmosphere I replied, 'It smells as if he is still here,' but Soapy gave me one of those blank looks beloved of his breed and I did

'I did warn you that a certain amount of redecorating was necessary'

not pursue the joke. Some people have no sense of humour.

Just then there was terrible rumbling noise from the garden and the house quite definitely moved.

'Good God,' I cried, 'the house is sliding about under our feet!'

Soapy behaved with considerable courage, although a trifle pale himself.

'I doubt very much if it actually *moved,* sir,' he said. 'Perhaps a trifle of settlement but no more. The trains occasionally cause a little vibration. One must expect a small amount of settlement in older property.'

We went upstairs where Soapy blushed deeply as he referred to the extra rooms which would be so useful if my lady-wife and I were to be blessed with more children. Mercifully he did not probe into the usual offices, which I have no doubt would have proved highly unusual.

However, I noticed that there was one room which he seemed to be deliberately avoiding. It was so plain he did not wish me to go in there that I pushed open the door and walked in myself. As I did so there was a terrible creaking noise and I sank through the floor.

Perhaps that is a slight exaggeration. At any rate a floorboard gave way and my left leg shot through up to the knee. I felt like Rumplestiltskin. Then the plaster underneath gave way and I sank up to my thigh in the middle of the floor.

As Soapy hauled me out he said: 'Of course, sir, I did warn you that a certain amount of redecoration was necessary.'

I returned home smelling like an old tomb.

April 14 Felt as stiff as if I had played rugby yesterday. Lucky it is Sunday. At lunchtime in The Crown Askew said I should always beware of property needing 'slight renovation'. He wrote out for me his private guide to estate agent's jargon, which I append.

ASKEW'S GUIDE

The property has been considerably renovated	A speculator has bought it, covered the cracks with paint, and is now asking two thousand quid more than it's worth.

Pebble dash elevations	Vast yawning cracks all over the front.
Exclusive development	The local authority stopped them cramming any more houses on the site.
Purpose-built to the highest standards	Nothing will actually go wrong until the builders have left.
Attractive, older-style property	A wreck
Cottage-style home	A wreck in a terrace
Town house	A modern wreck in a terrace
Partial central heating	A small rusty pipe in the hall which persistently dribbles.

We made so much noise compiling our list that the landlord asked us to be quiet. There was another type of property mentioned but Askew upset his beer over that sheet so we threw it away.

April 15 Newsagent delivered *The Times* today, instead of the *Telegraph.* Called in to exchange the paper on my way to work and he said I had cancelled the *Telegraph* because they didn't publish my letter. I wish I were not so impulsive.

April 16 There was an unfortunate incident when I called to look over a house this evening. Askew had advised me to pretend to be knowledgeable, as this convinces the vendor that you won't be fooled. On his recommendation, therefore, I took out my penknife and cut a tiny sliver of wood from the skirting board.

While I was pretending to examine it, and shaking my head, the owner snatched it from my hand and shouted, 'How dare you come here and without so much as a by-your-leave saw great chunks out of my skirting-board? Get out of the house at once!'

So much for Askew's wild wheezes.

April 17 Tried a new estate agent today. I left work early to get there before they closed. This whole business is not doing my work any good. Maureen, my secretary, says I look worried and preoccupied.

This agent proved the jovial type, all bounce and back-slapping, but his list is as useless as the others. We can't afford the good property and don't want the bad. However, there was one which interested us, a little detached house with two bedrooms and quite cheap.

April 18 Arranged to see the house on Saturday with Sheila. Sir Phillip entered my office as I was 'phoning and gave me a dark look. He is the sort of man who turns people into Communists.

April 19 I wish the newsagent would not keep delivering the *Daily Mail*. I left definite instructions that I wanted to go back to the *Telegraph*.

April 20 Sheila and I saw the little house and fell in love with it. It is one of those country relics you sometimes find in the suburbs, on a sort of island at the side of a big new estate.

It is very tall and thin, two-storeyed, with one big room downstairs and two bedrooms upstairs. There is a garage attached. They say it used to belong to the big house before it was pulled down. The roof is terribly picturesque, all uneven like you get with old cottages. There is a tiny garden with Virginia Creeper.

We made an offer £250 below the asking price. The agent rang us within half-an-hour to say the offer was accepted. The owner wishes a quick sale as he is going abroad.

April 21 Jack Askew says he knows a builder who will look over the house for us at a moderate fee and report.

April 22 Gaye arrived home from Norfolk today, ate a huge meal and says she is returning to University tomorrow.

April 23 Askew's builder friend, Mr. Orford, says he will look over the house for us and if we want anything doing he will be glad to quote. It will cost five guineas.

April 24 Gaye has not returned to University yet as she has become friendly with the Australian boys upstairs. The noise is indescribable but I can hardly complain as most of it is being made by my own daughter.

April 26 Today received following letter from Mr. Orford, the builder:

Dear Sir,

RE 46B ST. ANNES GROVE

Have inspected same and find as follows:

The property leans considerably to the left although this is compensated for by the fact that the garage leans to the right. There is central heating in every room but as far as I can discover there is no boiler in the house. A modern bathroom has been installed but there is nowhere for the water to run away. This, however, does not matter as the bathroom has been added without planning permission and will have to be pulled down anyway.

There is evidence of considerable rising damp in the walls. This is in danger of meeting the sinking damp coming down from where the guttering is defective. When this happens, the house will fall down, the same as when the whitlows meet round your waist.

In my opinion this house has been done up by a do-it-yourself expert with the intention of effecting a quick sale. I do not believe it would last a bad winter.

Yours faithfully,
C. Orford

I am in despair.

April 27 Someone has written on the lavatory wall of our Underground station: 'Tomorrow is cancelled through lack of interest.' I know how they feel.

April 28 Told the estate agent what the builder had said. I warned him if they were still advertising the property in a fortnight's time I would report the matter to the appropriate authorities. Then realised there *are* no appropriate authorities for estate agents. They may do as they please. I wish I had become one when I was demobbed from the Army.

April 29 Posted Mr. Orford five guineas. Allowing mileage at a shilling a mile I have spent £23 and 24 hours looking for somewhere to live. If I had spent that time studying the stock market I could be a rich man by now.

May 1 Uncle Walter says undertakers are the best estate agents. They can tip you off when someone dies and you swoop down before the owner's body is cold. Life is difficult enough without stupid suggestions like that.

Three

May 4 I feel there must be a great deal of wisdom in the text: 'Out of evil cometh good.'

Today I have become the owner of a house. Or at least, I have put down a few pounds as a token deposit with an agent, and will become the proprietor when I can raise the rest.

It is not the house we want. In fact it is not going too far to say it is the house we do *not* want. It is too large, and too old and the district isn't quite suitable but it is somewhere to live.

The house is in Broadwell Street, a terrace of rather run-down Victorian houses not far from the river. It is the only cheap house we have seen which is not falling down. At £4,500 it is reasonable by London standards.

Our choice was finally settled by Charles, a rather peculiar friend of Askew's. Charles dyes his hair and makes a living renovating old property. He is the sort of person who calls the living-room 'the conversation piazza' and the kitchen 'the food preparation area'.

Charles says it is a 'wonderful investment, duckie', as the district is sure to go up. We shall have to spend a few hundred on improvements but Charles says we can get a grant from the local council and easily borrow the rest.

'Promise to paint the front door yellow or I shall never

speak to you again, duckie,' said Charles, who has painted his own hair yellow.

Sheila feels the house is right for us. I am only relieved we don't have to tramp round any more derelict property.

May 5 Did not sleep last night. I was just about to drop off when I realised that I shall have to find more than £5,000. The thought of actually signing a cheque for £4,500 terrifies me. Spent most of the day asking other people if they had ever felt like this. To my relief, they all had. Unfortunately, every single person advised me against the purchase.

Maureen, my secretary, said the price is so cheap for a big house that I should check whether there is a sitting tenant there. She said her brother bought a house and after everything was signed they found an old man in the basement.

'He wouldn't go,' said Maureen, 'and wouldn't leave the house in case they locked him out and in the end they had to sell as he was driving them mad. He used to insist on paying his rent every day instead of weekly, and he used to totter up the stairs from the basement with 7s 1½d in his gnarled fist just as they sat down to supper.'

I have never felt more depressed in my life after hearing that story. Shall not sign a thing until I have searched the house from top to bottom.

May 6 Newsagent delivered the *Sun* today. As if I do not have enough worries.

May 8 I suppose I shall to face up to the financial implications of this reckless step. I have so far paid £10 to the vendor's agent as a gesture of good faith, but he wants me to make it up to ten per cent of the purchase price as soon as I can.

I think I can raise this by raiding all my savings and this will serve as a deposit if I get one of those ninety per cent mortgages everyone else seems to have. The money for the alterations I shall get partly from the local authority grant, and the bank should lend me the rest. It seems ominously simple.

Tonight I compiled the following sum:

Assets	£	s	d	*Expenditure*	£	s	d
Money in bldg. soc.	283	6	4	House (less £10)	4,490	–	–
Premium bonds	50	–	–	Alterations	700	–	–
Savings certs.	80	–	–	Legal	?	?	?
P.O. Savings Bank	53	7	8	Moving exps.	?	?	?
Money in pig	1	5	–	Carpets etc.	?	?	?
Wife's contribution	?	?	?	Sundries	?	?	?
Council grant	?	?	?				
Bldg. soc. loan	?	?	?				
Bank loan	?	?	?				
	?	?	?		?	?	?

Sheila says there are too many question marks.

May 9 I am glad the newsagent delivered the *Guardian* in error today, as it had a big advertisement by the Granite National Building Society.

It showed two people. On the left was Mr. Worried, who had never put money into a building society and who was being kicked out of his flat because they were pulling down the whole block. On the right Mr. Thriftwise, who had regularly saved with the building society and now they were giving him a fat mortgage to buy his own home.

My own savings are in the Granite National so I shall get the money from them. I suppose you just go in and see the genial manager who smiles out of the adverts.

May 10 Having completed the current issue of *The Condenser* left the office early and called at our local office of the Granite National just before they closed and asked to see the genial manager. He had gone home.

May 11 Called at building society this morning (Saturday) and asked to see the genial manager, but he does not come in on Saturday mornings. I do not know when they expect me to see him. Am I supposed to wait for my August holidays?

May 13 Rang building society and made an appointment to see the genial manager the day after tomorrow at 5.15. He tried to make it earlier but I was insistent. I cannot keep sneaking away from the office like this. The whole office know about my search for a home. Nobby, the commissionaire, tells them. Like all old soldiers he has a sixth sense for rumour.

May 15 Saw building society manager. He did not look like the genial fellow in their advertisements. He was tall and bald and his hands quivered and he appeared to be half-witted. At any rate he shook hands with a grip like a tired snake and said, 'Sit down, Mr. Etherington.'

I said, 'I am not Mr. Etherington,' whereupon he became angry and said, 'Well you should be. It is in my diary here—Mr. Etherington 5.15. This is most upsetting. I have waited behind specially.'

Thinking to introduce a lighter note into the proceedings I replied, 'I am really Mr. Thriftwise!'

He stared at me and said: 'Who is Mr. Thriftwise?'

I handed him a copy of the advertisement from the *Guardian* and he remarked, 'This is news to me. We never know what Head Office is going to do next. At any rate, now you are here, what do you want?'

I told him I wanted a mortgage. For a moment I thought he was going to have a seizure, but then he took off his glasses and stared at me for a long time before saying, 'Aren't you rather old?'

This was in such contrast to the treatment Mr. Thriftwise received that I could not reply properly, but stammered out that I was only 47. He asked me what I did for a living and I said I was a journalist, adding: 'I am editor of *The Condenser*. I expect you have heard of it.'

He had not even heard of *The Condenser*. He entered into a long diatribe about how careful the society had to be about lending money to elderly people with irregular jobs such as

'I am really Mr. Thriftwise'

journalists. When I could slide a word in I said, 'But I am an investor. I have money in the Society.' He said that did not make any difference.

As it was obvious he was not going to lend me any money I left at the end of one of his interminable anecdotes. After going I found I had left my hat behind but nothing would induce me to return for it.

Sheila would not believe a word of my story and kept pointing to the advertisement.

'You must have offended him in some way,' she said. 'I am sure they would not print advertisements like this unless they were true.'

May 16 Wrote to manager of the Granite National Building Society and withdrew my £283 6s 4d stating that I was sure he would understand why. Also asked for return of hat.

May 19 Called at East Sheen Building Society. They will not lend money on property over 50 years old.

May 22 Saw Midland Provident Building Society. They will not lend money to people over 40 unless they put down half the purchase price.

May 24 Received a letter (and my money) from the Granite National manager saying he could not understand why I was withdrawing my account and they always tried to give satisfaction. The man is a charlatan. They did not enclose my hat.

May 25 West Surrey Building Society require a fifty per cent deposit on property over thirty years old. The manager said 'Between you and me, sir, we are not very keen on this sort of business.'

May 26 The Lower Gornal Building Society want a forty per cent deposit because I am so old. I have never felt so decrepit in my life. Until last week I considered myself a particularly fit person. I always have to wait for Jack Askew to climb the hill at the thirteenth. I asked Maureen at the office if I really looked old and she said anyone over 25 looks old to her anyway.

May 28 Am in some difficulty about the money I withdrew from the Granite National. I intended to deposit it with the society which grants me a mortgage, but I can't find one.

May 31 Deposited money from Granite National with the East Hammersmith and Shepherd's Bush Building Society. They will not give me a mortgage. I am now convinced that building societies exist for the sole purpose of obstructing members of the public who wish to buy their own houses. They will not lend money unless you are a 30-year-old Civil Servant with a large private income. In other words, someone like Burgess and Maclean, the defecting diplomats. I bet *they* never had any trouble with a mortgage.

June 1 Estate agents today threatened to cancel sale unless I cough up 10 p.c. deposit. Askew says it is time I saw a solicitor. I don't think I have ever been to see a solicitor in my life. Askew recommends his friend, Atkins.

'He is a commissioner for oaths,' said Askew mysteriously. I certainly feel like swearing.

June 2 Telephoned Atkins today (from office). Sir Phillip came sneaking in just as I finished. I believe he was listening outside the door.

Atkins said he would be delighted to act for me, although he could not remember who Jack Askew is. He also offered to act for the vendor as well. This seems rather strange. He says he can arrange a mortgage with the East Bromsgrove Building Society, for whom he happens to be an agent.

June 3 Left office early and saw Atkins who says I can leave everything in his hands. I am most impressed—he seems to know what he is doing.

June 4 Filled in building society forms. All is in the capable hands of Atkins. Can at last concentrate on earning my living.

June 5 Gaye sent us letter demanding money. She has spent her allowance on travelling to Reading to demonstrate in support of student independence. I wrote and suggested she showed her independence of the guilty older generation by paying her own fare.

June 6 (anniversary of D-Day): During the night decided I had been mean to Gaye and posted her a few pounds in a.m. When I told Sheila in p.m. she said she had also sent money to Gaye as she thought I was not going to do so. So the wretched girl now has twice what she asked for and we shall be living on cheese and pickles for a fortnight.

June 7 No news of house.

June 8 Sir Phillip called me into his office today and said he was worried at the number of mistakes in the last issue of *The Condenser*. I don't wonder—all energies have been concentrated on trying to buy a house.

June 9 When I told Nobby, the commissionaire, that I thought our new district would go up he said his brother-in-law bought a house by a cricket field and six months later they built a riveting works there.

June 10 No acknowledgement from Gaye of money.

June 11 Received mysterious package through post containing advertisement material for life insurance and pension schemes. Burned it.

June 12 Further mysterious package received. This time for householders comprehensive through the West Leek Mutual Provident Fund. Burned.

June 13 What is going on? My mail this morning contained a stream of advertising material, namely: A handbill from a firm of insurance brokers; a leaflet from the Professional People's Provident Fund; a positive book from the Amalgamated Unit Trust; and a pamphlet from a building society. I wish I could discover who has given these people my address.

June 14 East Bromsgrove Building Society telephoned today to say their surveyor had been to the address given by Mr. Atkins and it was the wrong house. Gave them right address.

June 15 No letter from Gaye. Advertisement circular from the Republican Assurance Society received, asking if I looked forward to starving in my old age or would I prefer to retire with £20,000? There was a picture on the front of some old idiot pruning his roses. Fools.

June 16 Wrote to Gaye and asked if she received money.

June 17 Sir Phillip has circulated another office memo about the use of the telephone for private calls. I am very worried because Maureen rings up boy friends on my extension and with this house there are too many private calls already.

June 18 We are trying to save money in view of the new house but this evening I took ten shillings from the telephone tin to have a drink with Jack Askew. Unfortunately Sheila heard me getting out the money so I had to put it back.

June 19 Received letter from building society enclosing a bill for their surveyor (ten guineas) and a further bill for five guineas for 'abortive visit to wrong address'. I immediately rang Atkins and asked if he was going to pay the five guineas as he had sent them to the wrong place. He said he wasn't.

He then said: 'Did you receive all the correspondence I sent you?'

I asked him what correspondence and he said *the literature relating to insurance, unit trusts and pensions.*

His insolence took my breath away. He calmly went on to say he was an agent for these people as well as for the building society and he thought I might be interested.

'If you had taken out a with-profits policy twenty years ago you would be rich today,' he told me.

I told him that if he was really concerned about my financial welfare he could pay the five guineas extra fee for the surveyor. He laughed.

June 20 Jack Askew says a building society only survey a property for valuation. I should have the house independently surveyed if I am having building work done. He knows a retired surveyor who will do it for me cheap.

June 21 Postcard received from Gaye not mentioning money.

June 22 Spoke to Maureen about using office 'phone for private calls. She told me eavesdroppers never hear good of themselves. I cannot see what that has to do with it.

June 25 Further morbid pamphlet received from insurance company with a drawing of a woman sitting by the fire and a blank space in the chair opposite. The pamphlet asked: 'What would your wife do if you died tomorrow?' I felt like replying, 'Laugh her head off.' Obviously more of Atkins' work. This constant harping on old age and death is wearing me down.

June 27 By first post received report from Askew's surveyor. To my utter dismay, he says the house is falling down! At least, that is the impression from his report, which is couched in jargon incomprehensible to an ordinary person.

It appears there is a fracture over the porch . . . the brickwork is laminated . . . the plinth is breaking away . . . there is a fracture in the rendering . . . the flashings are loose . . . the fixing of the main purlin is defective . . . woodworm has attacked the stairs . . . and the house is riddled with something called Dote.

He adds that the larder in the kitchen is unsatisfactory because it is warm and that on trying to test the electricity supply he received a shock from the main switch. He values the house at £700 below what we are paying.

A footnote says he could not get into roof owing to his age, weight and heart condition.

June 28 Withdrew our offer on the house and sent the owner a copy of the surveyor's report.

June 29 Received angry 'phone call from owner of house.

'You can tell that surveyor from me,' he shouted, 'that I personally fixed that electric wiring myself, so if he got a shock it's his own fault. And as regards the larder being warm, kindly tell him that was the airing-cupboard, not the larder.'

June 30 Rang surveyor with owner's comments. The surveyor said he was sorry I had withdrawn my offer.

I said what about the dreaded Dote, woodworm and so forth. He said ,'Oh, that's all right. My own house is a heaving mass of woodworm. As long as the staircase isn't actually moving it's O.K.'

I asked him if his report was really meant to be favourable and he replied, 'Oh yes, I thought I made it quite clear. You mustn't pay too much attention to all the little things wrong.'

Am I living in a madhouse? Here is a man charging me 25 guineas to ignore his report. However, we have no choice but to ask if we can withdraw the withdrawal of our offer.

July 1 The owner of the house adopted a high tone, he didn't like being mucked around like this, etc., etc. Was forced to humiliate myself, but in the end he agreed to let the original offer stand.

July 2 Noticed grey streak in hair. Letter from Gaye asking for more money. She has not acknowledged the first lot yet. I cannot think whom she takes after. Certainly not my side of the family, although mother had a cousin who ended in Carey Street.

July 3 Received letter from building society who offer to advance only £3,200 on the house. This is not enough. Telephoned Atkins for his advice but was unable to speak to him as his assistant says he is very busy. Sending out insurance leaflets, I suppose.

July 4 Atkins away 'inspecting property'.

July 5 Had embarrassing experience in Grosvenor Square. Met an old friend I hadn't seen for years and asked him, 'What happened to that fat girl at the tennis club who everyone hated?' He said, 'I married her.'

July 8 Cannot contact Atkins. Have left five messages for him to ring me without any result. I should like to get the sale through before we go on holiday.

July 9 Sir Phillip came into my office today to make sure that his daughter's wedding is reported in *The Condenser*. He asked if I felt all right, as I had appeared a bit preoccupied recently.

July 14 I have given up hope of anything happening before the holidays. We go next week with Jack and Freda Askew to Salcombe for a fortnight. Gaye arrived home from University today, ate a pound of the finest steak, broke a valuable vase and left the immersion heater on all afternoon.

Tomorrow she goes grape-picking in the South of France. God help the French. Sheila is worried that 'something might happen to her' while she is in France. Personally I feel if anything is going to happen to that girl it is much more likely to occur at that University, judging by the company there.

July 19 No news. We leave for Salcombe tomorrow. I shall not keep a diary while on holiday.

Four

July 23 Although I said I would not keep a diary on holiday I find it difficult to break the habit. Must record an interesting thing—Askew and I have found a pub where you can drink after hours. Won four bob at golf today and had a row with the secretary of the club who complained about Askew jumping up and down on the greens. Askew told him he was chasing a snake.

July 29 Am keeping resolution not to keep diary.

August 3 Returned home from Salcombe. No news of house.

August 5 Rang Atkins. Unable to speak to him so left strong message asking him to ring me.

August 7 To my surprise Atkins rang me at the office. He had the insolence to say he *has been trying to get hold of me but I am so elusive ha ha.* Will I please send him £440 at once as he wants to exchange contracts, whatever that means. He says it means that if I back out now I forfeit the money. Oh God, what have I done?

Told him I had been trying to contact him because the building society are only offering £3,200, which leaves me £1,300 short. He said I should have thought of that before.

August 8 By withdrawing nearly every penny of our savings (except the money in the pig) I have raised £440. I am particularly upset at cashing the premium bonds, as they had never won a prize. Sent cheque to Atkins. We must not weaken now.

August 9 While Sheila and I were watching television a middle-aged couple knocked at the door and said they had come to look at the flat. We said there must be some mistake but they said no, the agents had sent them to this address as the lease was not being renewed in September.

With alarm I realised that the lease did indeed expire then. I had assumed we should have been in our own home by September. Told the couple there must have been a mistake and they went away extremely angry.

August 10 When I told the agents I was not renewing the lease earlier this year I remember being rather rude. So today I wrote a humble letter apologising for my earlier curtness, saying I had been under strain, etc., and could we renew for a year only?

August 12 Agents wrote to say they were deeply relieved to hear I was no longer under strain but the the lease must be renewed for three years at the increased rent. This means we shall have to find new tenants when we move into the new house. As if we did not have enough problems. There are times when I feel Job was a much overrated person.

August 13 Gaye arrived back from France looking as if she had not washed for a month. She wore no shoes and hardly any clothes except a few tattered rags. However, I may look like that myself soon.

August 14 There was a list of winning premium bonds in the paper. Sheila says she recognises one of the numbers as ours but we cannot be sure as we have sold the bonds. It would have won £500. In future we shall not look at the winners.

August 15 A rough calculation of our finances reveals the following:

Assets	£	s	d	*Liabilities*	£ s d
Money in bldg. soc.	0	0	0	Balance to find on house	1,000 (approx.)
Premium bonds	0	0	0	Legal fees	50 (?)
Savings certs.	0	0	0		
P.O. Savings Bank	0	0	0		
Money in pig	2	3	4		
Wife's assets (she says)	81	5	6		
	£83	8	10		£1,050

Deficiency: £966 11s 2d.

I have made no mention of moving, decorating and building alterations in this sum as all energies are concentrated on the apparently insuperable problems of buying the place.

Sheila says what about that £966 11s 2d? Indeed.

August 16 This morning I went to the firm's accountant and told him I want to commute my pension. It is a voluntary scheme so I am able to do this. I shall get back about £1,100 in contributions which will enable us to keep our heads above water. The accountant says I am being very foolish.

August 17 By a weird coincidence one of Atkins's leaflets arrived this morning. It showed a seedy-looking man saying to a worn-out woman: 'Without a pension I really do not know what we are going to do.' I wish he would stop sending these things and get on with the purchase of the house.

August 18 Sir Phillip called me in to his office today. He says he is very disturbed to hear I am commuting my pension.

'It is none of my business what you do with your pension,' he said, 'but we are a firm who demand loyalty.'

He is convinced I am planning to leave. I told him the facts but he believes I am laying some deep plot. This afternoon he suddenly opened my office door and stared at me for ten seconds before withdrawing.

August 19 Rang Atkins, but unable to speak to him. As I was on the 'phone the door opened and Sir Phillip stood there. He said: 'There seems to be a lot of telephoning in this office, ha, ha,' and left.

August 20 Jack Askew said tonight that I ought to take Atkins out to lunch as that might hurry things up. I have never heard anything more immoral in my life, this suggestion that a member of a respectable profession has to be bribed with food and drink to do his job properly. Eight months ago I would have dismissed the idea completely.

August 21 Rang Atkins. As usual not able to speak to him so I said: 'Tell him I want to invite him to lunch with me.'

The clerk put his hand over the 'phone and I heard him say in muffled tones, 'He says he wants to buy you lunch.'

I did not catch the reply but the clerk then told me, 'He's just come in,' and this was followed by Atkins's booming tones of fake joviality.

I suggested a restaurant near his office but he said, 'Oh no, not there, it's a crummy place. Let's go to L'Escargot d'Or.' His insolence deprived me of speech, otherwise I would have pointed out that the host usually chooses the venue. Besides, the Cargo of Whores (as Askew calls it) is the most expensive place for miles around.

August 23 Met Atkins for lunch. He kept me waiting half an hour at the restaurant. It is one of those places in total darkness, with a menu the length of your arm. There appears to be no kitchen—at any rate, all food is cooked on a spirit stove by your elbow, so conversation is punctuated by great sheets of flame.

Atkins amused me by telling me of his clients. 'Three of them got twelve years yesterday,' he said. 'Mind you, I got my fee out of them before the trial.' He did not mention any successful defences.

I tried to steer Atkins round to the possibility of expediting the house purchase but he said conveyancing could not be hurried.

'The game is not worth the candle,' he said. 'Most solicitors cannot make ends meet on the miserable scale of fees allowed.'

As Atkins was drinking his second brandy the bill arrived. It was as long as the menu, which is saying a great deal. All wasted money. Atkins thanked me charmingly and said, 'We must do this again some time.' He then left in a taxi to sue a stricken widow.

August 26 As the weather is warm the Australian boys held an all-day beer and rave with the windows open. They invited Gaye. The noise was indescribable. Five people complained.

August 28 Met one of the Australian boys on the stairs and he thanked me for not complaining the other day. He asked me if Gaye got home all right.

I asked what he meant and he said, 'She threw up about half past seven and some joker said he would take her back home.' As Gaye had not arrived home until 3 a.m. this item of news hardly soothed me.

August 31 When I tried to 'phone Atkins today the switchboard operator asked, 'Is it a private call?' I fear Sir Phillip is on my track. He has a strange look in his eye these days and a habit of regarding me sideways.

September 1 It is now eight months since I decided to buy a house and I do not even own so much as a brick. I shall not write any more in my diary until I hear something definite. I shall not try to telephone Atkins again. I dare not even think of the building work. As Uncle Walter said recently, 'Learn to dread one day at a time.'

October 2 Have heard from Atkins. He is now ready to complete, and will send me the details. I was so pleased that I took Sheila out to dinner.

October 3 I wish to know if it is possible to sue a solicitor. Atkins has now completed, and the house is mine upon payment of his bill and the balance needed by the building society. After detailing the scale fee for the conveyance, together with search fees and so on, he has the impudence to add the following:

To miscellaneous telephone calls etc.	£14	18s	4d
Various petty disbursements	£11	19s	7d
Lunch	£5	5s	0d
Taxi		10s	0d

In addition he has the incompetence to make an error of £1,000 in the purchase price of the house.

I was so distressed when I opened the letter that it was only by a great effort I restrained myself from going round to Atkins's office and throwing a brick through the window. Instead, I went down to The Crown and got drunk.

October 4 Awoke with vile headache. Rang Atkins and was told as usual that he was out. I said I wished to speak to him urgently about lunch and that drew him to the 'phone. I then told him: 'Look here, about this bill you have sent, I refuse to pay it.'

He replied, 'Well, until you do, you won't be able to buy the house. I'm in no hurry.'

I asked him how he arrived at the figure of £14 18s 4d for miscellaneous 'phone calls and he said it was based on a calculation of his time at 6s 8d a call. 'It's your fault for being so elusive,' he said.

I decided to play my trump card and said, 'How dare you charge me five guineas for a lunch which I paid for, and then charge me ten shillings for *your* taxi?'

Atkins said, 'What's the matter? Didn't you enjoy the meal? I thought it was one of the best lunches I have ever had.'

I pointed out that he seemed to forget *I* had paid for it, and he replied, 'You merely paid for the food and drink. I am charging for the time taken. You must remember I am a very busy man.'

'Obviously,' I said triumphantly. 'So busy you that made a mistake of £1,000 in the price of the house.'

'I am glad you mentioned that,' he said. 'I will send you an amended account tomorrow but I shall have to charge for making an alteration in the contract.'

Further argument being impossible, I shouted down the 'phone, 'You make Dodson and Fogg look like a couple of saints!'

'I don't know Dodson and Fogg,' said Atkins calmly, 'but I don't doubt they're a very good firm.'

Spent the rest of the day trying to think of a way round Atkins but it is impossible. I cannot buy the house until I pay his bill as all money passes through his hands, and the ridiculous state of the law allows him to do what he likes.

October 5 Received a new statement from Atkins, correcting the mistake which I pointed out to him and charging an extra guinea 'for amending statement of account'. I will die rather than pay.

October 6 Paid Atkins. Would not have done it but for Sheila who said that if I don't pay Atkins I not only lose the chance of this house but forfeit the money already deposited. To think I spent five years as a ranker in the Army during the war defending among other things this crazy legal system. When I wrote out the cheque I deliberately made the writing as indistinct as possible.

October 9 Received receipt from Atkins, the keys of the house, and the news it is at last ours.

October 10 Forgot to mention earlier that Uncle Walter, from Harrow, recommended a little man who might do the building for us. He repaired Uncle Walter's concrete path. Uncle Walter asked him if he would do our job and he said he would be delighted. His name is Mr. Flamewell. Askew's builder-friend, Mr. Orford, is now bankrupt.

October 12 Sheila and I went to inspect the house in Broadwell St. today to see what needs doing. Unfortunately Askew and Uncle Walter both insisted on coming along. We found great difficulty in opening the front door, which Askew said had jammed because the foundations had slipped.

However, we found it was merely blocked by a great heap of advertisement circulars, mini-cab numbers and so forth, which were heaped behind it. There were also about seventy letters addressed to occupier and a card asking if I was saved.

It was very depressing inside the house, which also looks much smaller than it did. There was a terrible damp smell. It was raining and we could hear water dripping somewhere. Sheila says she knows someone died there, she can sense it. Uncle Walter says this house was built when they were using the last of the clay in the old London stock brickworks and as a result it will soon fall down. Askew says it would be better to tear out the entire inside and start again.

I searched the house from top to bottom to see if any sitting tenant had been left behind but there appears to be no one.

As we left the house a lace curtain twitched opposite and an inexpressibly evil face leered at us. It belonged to an old woman. I do hope the neighbours are not going to be unpleasant.

Afterwards we went into the pub on the corner. I have always wanted to live in a house with a pub on the corner. We waited for five minutes but nobody appeared to be serving so we moved into the lounge, only to find that the landlord had moved into the saloon.

I tapped on the counter with a coin to attract his attention and he came rushing into the lounge shouting, 'Don't keep banging the counter like that, you won't get served any quicker. You want serving in two seconds, that's your trouble.'

I told him that if he didn't want to serve me he needn't and went to walk out. He then shouted, 'That's right, go off in a huff just because I'm short-handed.'

Ordered a pint each for Askew and myself, a Scotch for Uncle Walter and a shandy for Sheila. Both pints were undrinkable, extremely cloudy with little bits floating in them, and my glass had a lipstick stain. I held it up to the light and the landlord said quickly, 'You won't find anything wrong with that.' Askew said no, and he wouldn't find much right with it either.

A little man in the corner said, 'He's a rare character is Bert, he won't stand no nonsense from anyone, he won't.' I hope *he* is not a typical customer.

October 13 Rang Flamewell, the builder, and arranged to meet him at the house. Flamewell's telephone appeared to be inside a concrete mixer judging by the noise, and I was obliged to shout. I was bellowing at my loudest when Sir Phillip came in and asked what all the row was about. Nobby, the commissionaire, said he could hear me in the corridor. Must be more careful.

October 15 Left work early on pretence of going to the printers, and met Flamewell at the house. Flamewell says it is a well-built house. He said the kitchen, which sticks out at the back, will have to come down and be rebuilt. The electricity board will never pass the wiring which is prehistoric, as is the gas installation. He will convert a bedroom into a bathroom and persuaded me to have the two downstairs rooms knocked into one. I showed him the surveyor's report which he dismissed as a load of old rubbish. He says surveyors do not know what they are talking about. I feel I shall get on well with Flamewell.

October 14 Flamewell rang to say that while he was doing the job, would I like him to put in a little fountain in the garden? He could recommend a cheap one with a gnome on top with water coming out of the top of his hat. Said I could not afford it.

October 17 Flamewell's estimate has arrived. Very reasonable—about £750 for everything. From that we can deduct the local authority grant (say £300). I shall have to borrow some money, of course, but am hoping the bank will help. After all, I have been a customer there for 23 years. Wrote to Flamewell, accepting his estimate.

October 19 Sheila says that as we are going to be short of money she will take a temporary job through a secretarial agency, as long as she can find a place where they don't need good shorthand as she never did master Pitman's. She is a good girl.

October 21 Flamewell has replied to my letter in handwriting so bad I was forced to ring him up to find out what he meant. He says before he can go ahead plans must be approved by the local authority. There should be no trouble as he knows the surveyor well. But I shall have to apply for the grant myself.

October 22 Askew's friend, Charles, says the way to improve old property is to make it look really old. He claims to have spent £500 half-wrecking a perfectly sound Georgian cottage so it looked quaint. Unfortunately he overdid it, and the place fell down.

October 23 Sheila collected form for improvement grant from the Town Hall. I cannot answer half the questions. They want to know of what material the foundations will be and such details. I sent the form to Flamewell already signed, and asked him to fill it in and send it off.

October 24 The agency have got a job for Sheila at the Fido Pet Food Factory in the Great West Road. We had an argument as to whether to put her wages in the pig or the bank. Sheila says if we put it in the pig I or Gaye will get at it. I say if we put it in the bank all three of us will get at it. Eventually we decided to put it in the building society.

October 26 Have been trying to contact Flamewell but can get no sense from a half-witted youth at his office. It seems he is converting a laundromat on the Edgware Road.

October 28 Went and looked at the house this evening. Nothing has changed. It seems to rain permanently in the neighbourhood. I was aware of staring eyes following me down the street. Felt like a criminal.

Dropped in at the pub on the corner which, by the way, is called The Spread Eagle. This time the landlord greeted me with heavy wit, i.e. 'Hullo, hullo, hullo, here comes that chap that's always complaining about something. What have you come to complain about tonight, eh?' Roars of sycophantic laughter greeted this sally from the morons in the saloon.

The little man in the corner (who, by the by, I now notice has only one leg) said Bert was a real character, wasn't he, he made you feel cheerful whatever the weather. I came near to striking a cripple for the first time in my life.

I shall certainly miss The Crown. However, I suppose there are more important things in life than having a nice pub just around the corner, although I can't think of any at the moment.

October 30 Flamewell rang to say he has sent off the form for the grant, and would I let him have a key to the house so he can admit the building inspector. He cannot start work until the grant is approved but at last things seem to be moving.

Bombarding the gardens with rockets and roman candles

Five

November 5 (Bonfire Night): Went to Jack Askew's firework party. There were tears among the children because the grown-ups monopolised all the fireworks. Sheila said she had never realised men could be so childish. I quite agree. Askew insisted on keeping all the rockets to himself. Askew's son lit a jumping jack which exploded up his mother's skirt. I laughed so much I had to go and hide behind a tree.

When we got home we were astonished to see sheets of flame coming out of the upper floors of the flats. Apparently the Australian boys were having a firework party inside the flat, bombarding the gardens with rockets and roman candles. How thankful I am that we shall be able to move soon.

November 6 Askew's friend, Charles, says a good name is essential for a house. He wants us to call the new place The Moorings. I explained we were half a mile from the river. He said there has never yet been a recorded case of houses called The Moorings having anything to do with boats.

November 22 Have been unable to write my diary for some time owing to a ghastly experience. Visiting Broadwell Street last week during the customary monsoon I noticed a large patch of damp on a bedroom ceiling. There was no

Momentarily suspended by his chinstrap

ladder to the loft but I managed to get in by standing on an old box and hauling myself up. I didn't have a torch and while I was groping among the rafters I slipped through them, twisting my knee and doing something nasty to my wrist and hand.

Owing to my injuries it was impossible to get down from the loft. After half an hour of futile attempts I feared I should never be found and die of starvation. Thought of crawling into the loft next door but that proved impossible.

Then I hit on the idea of prising loose a slate and hurling a message from the roof. I wrote: 'Fetch help. I am trapped in the roof of No. 13,' crawled to the side of the loft, where the roof slopes down, punched out two or three slates and hurled the piece of paper into the road.

The first time it blew away and landed in a gutter so I wrote another note and wrapped it round a piece of plaster. I also wrote another note (in case I should not be found in time), i.e. 'The insurance policy is in the left-hand drawer of the bureau,' which I tucked in my collar. I then composed myself for whatever fate had in store for me.

About fifteen minutes later there was a loud crash below and the sound of footsteps on the stairs. I shouted out and a policeman stuck his head through the trapdoor. Before I could thank him for coming he waved a truncheon at me and shouted, 'Come quietly, or we will fetch you down. And stop throwing slates all over the street. You might have killed someone. You drug addicts ought to be locked up.'

I said: 'No drug orgy is going on. I am the owner of this house. I have just put my fist through the ceiling. Thank heavens you got my message.'

He replied: 'I shall put *my* fist through something if you don't come down,' and started to hoist himself through the hatch. Unfortunately he slipped while doing so and fell back through the hole, his helmet catching on the sides, so he was momentarily suspended by his chinstrap.

After about ten minutes I was able to convince him that I was entitled to be there. A woman living opposite had seen the slates flying into the street and called the police. No one had found my message which I later discovered in the front garden. The police gave me a lift home, which was the least they could do considering they had done ten pounds' damage to the front door.

November 23 Rang Flamewell re grant. He says it must have missed the November meeting of the Council Finance Committee.

November 24 Sheila has been sacked from the pet food factory. Apparently she made a mistake in a letter as a result of which eight crates of cat food were sent to Lundy Island. She says the real reason is that the sales manager wants someone younger as he likes to make passes at the teenage girls. However, the agency will soon find something.

November 27 I have been brooding over the pet food sales manager and I have half a mind to write to him and ask him what he means by not finding my wife attractive enough to assault. However, Sheila has now started at XYZ Electronics. She has not yet found out what they make, but she says it is something to do with valves.

December 1 I have had to remake the front page of the Christmas issue of *The Condenser* as Sir Phillip wants a special message inserting.

It is headed 'Yuletide Greetings from the Chairman' and contains heavy references to the season of goodwill and pulling together, etc. etc. I can think of nothing more calculated to cause a strike. I put it in black type with a border of holly round the edge.

December 7 Sure enough, the works at Wolverhampton *have* gone on strike. They have discovered that the special Christmas dinner in the canteen which is costing 4s 6d is being served free in the managerial dining-room. Sir Phillip has decided to withdraw his Christmas message as a punishment. I have replaced it with a cartoon from an agency.

December 9 I believe Sir Phillip thinks I fomented the strike. He looks at me very oddly these days.

December 12 Rang Town Hall and asked if the Committee had approved my grant yet. They told me the Committee does not meet this month owing to Christmas. I was so angry that I banged down the telephone and broke the receiver. Fortunately I was 'phoning from the office. I made a temporary repair with some sticky tape but there is now a loud hissing in the earpiece.

December 13 Maureen said today, 'The cleaners broke your 'phone overnight and tried to mend it with sticky plaster.' I feigned indignation.

December 14 Nobby, the commissionaire, says he ticked off the cleaner re the 'phone.

December 15 While I was sitting late in the office, trying to make up work lost through the house, the door burst open and a middle-aged woman with a cigarette dangling from her mouth burst in and asked what I meant by accusing her of wrecking all the telephones? She'd have the law on me, etc., etc., I had no right to say things like that about people.

I told her we had now discovered who broke the 'phone but she refused to be pacified and said she would not work here any more. When I got home my supper had all dried up into a desiccated mound.

December 16 Gaye arrived home from University today and reduced the flat to a holocaust in ten minutes.

December 23 When I got home there was no sign of Sheila but I did not worry as I knew they had an office Christmas party at XYZ Electronics. She had left a stew in the oven. At eight o'clock I was beginning to feel rather worried when there was a knock at the door and there was my wife, looking as pale as a sheet and supported by two men.

They said she had been taken ill at the party. I replied, 'Alcoholic poisoning, I should think,' and Sheila muttered something to the effect that they were to pay no attention to *him*, if anyone ought to know the symptoms of alcoholic poisoning it was her husband, etc., etc. She then lurched into the kitchen, pulled the stew from the oven and dropped it all over the floor. I have never felt so embarrassed in all my life.

December 24 During the night Sheila woke in tears and said she would never forgive herself, if there was one thing she despised it was a drunk woman, fancy being brought home in that state by two men and so forth. She kept me awake all night with remorse.

Had our own office party at lunch-time. I find them a bore these days. Must be getting old. Went into my office about three to 'phone and found Maureen sprawled on my desk with a young lad from the Wages Dept.

Neither made any attempt to move so I had to 'phone from another office. When I returned I was horrified to see Sir Phillip look into my room. I don't know his reaction as I tip-toed away and hid.

December 25 (Quarter Day): As usual, a day of bloated gloom. I spent too long at The Crown at lunch-time and Sheila did her martyr's act when I returned. She said the bird was ruined but personally I have never properly tasted the bird in twenty-odd years of marriage. I am more and more convinced that Scrooge was one of the most sensible men I have ever read about.

However, when the effects of the midday feast wore off we had quite a pleasant evening. Played Scrabble but Gaye kept introducing medical terms of a lewd nature. She says I am inhibited.

January 1 It is now twelve months since I decided to buy a house and I am still not living in it. I cannot understand why such a basic thing should be so complicated. No wonder the country has a debit balance of payments. My New Year resolution would be to burn my diary, but this year I have been given seven.

January 4 Gaye keeps asking, 'Have you put anything in my diary yet?'

January 16 Glad I didn't burn my diary because things are moving again. The council have approved my grant subject to some conditions which Flamewell is looking into. Flamewell says the grant is £312 5s 7d and it would have been less if he didn't know the building inspector. Hooray!

January 18 We had another circular sent round the office today, signed by Sir Phillip, stating that any employee found making personal 'phone calls would be instantly dismissed. Was it coincidence that there were two copies of the memorandum in my envelope?

I assume this directive does not apply to Sir Phillip himself, who is usually on the 'phone to his bookmaker whenever I enter his office. But I must be careful. It is this wretched house.

January 19 Received letter confirming grant. But it is conditional on the following work being done: damp-proof course inserted all round; garden wall rebuilt; door leading from kitchen to outside lavatory to be locked up and a new door cut in the wall; overflow pipe to be moved; and various other adjustments.

I asked Flamewell how much the extra work would cost and he estimated £300. I pointed out that the grant itself was only £312 so that in effect my grant was being reduced to £12 and he said yes, it seemed hard, but that was life wasn't it.

Is it too late to emigrate to Australia at my age? I am becoming convinced this country is run by insane people.

January 20

FINANCIAL STATEMENT

Assets	£	s	d	*Liabilities*	£	s	d
Sundry (including money saved from Sheila's wages)	73	1	–	Cost of conversion	750	–	–
Grant	312	–	–	Extra work to get grant	300	–	–
	385	1	–		1,050	–	–

Fortunately the grant will give me a breathing-space. I wonder when it will arrive.

January 21 Flamewell rang up and said he was all ready to start but would I first pay him £300? I asked him what for, and he said he couldn't carry me, he had to buy timber and various materials.

I said I would pay him when I got the grant and he said, 'Don't you know, you don't get the grant until the work is finished? You ought to read the small print.'

I did so and he is right. That means I have to find £300 before work can begin. I shall try the bank.

January 22 Rang bank manager and fixed appointment. Like the building society manager he does not come in on Saturday mornings and leaves the office every day at 4.30, so I shall just have to take time off work. But beggars can't be choosers. I shall take some work on *The Condenser* home with me.

January 23 Saw bank manager. Although I have been a customer for many years he obviously hasn't the faintest idea who I am. He kept me waiting half an hour and then ushered me into his office and asked what could he do for me, Mr. Er—er. I said he could lend me £300 for a start.

I have never seen a person's expression change so rapidly. It was as if he had seen something unspeakably vile crawling across the floor. I hurriedly put in that I wanted the money to improve an old house, in line with current Government policy, and that I had been a customer for fifteen years without ever having overdrawn.

He got out a little card which presumably contained my financial biography and peered at it and then he asked if I could put up security to cover a loan? I pointed out that if I had security for £300 I wouldn't need to borrow the money. As he still looked as if the carpet smelt I said he could have the deeds of the house.

He replied, 'Yes, they might be sufficient provided that the house is in good repair.'

I explained I couldn't put the house in good repair until he lent me the money and he said, 'Then I'm afraid you must cut your coat according to your cloth.'

I reminded him that his bank were currently conducting an advertising campaign with the slogan 'The Bank That Cares', but I was obviously wasting my time. He had not even read the advertisement. They obviously *don't* care. Left his door open as I went out but had to return for my hat. The manager said, 'Good morning, what can I do for you?'

January 24 Sent following letter to bank manager:

Dear Pecksniff,

With reference to your peremptory dismissal of my request for a loan to put a roof over my head:

I would remind you that at a time when the Chancellor is trying to curb lending for non-essential matters you have introduced a credit card scheme to encourage people to guzzle without thought of the morrow. And while I am refused a loan not a day passes without some cheap business crook going bankrupt, the chief creditors inevitably being the banks. I saw in yesterday's *Times* that you lent £30,000 to some plausible rogue who was justly sentenced to five years.

I have been a customer for 23 years, in which time I have received six wrong statements and three times have been debited for cheques which I did not even issue. My attempts to enter your unit trust scheme were frustrated by your predecessor who advised me to put all my money in a building society. Had I not done so I would today be a comparatively wealthy man. I can only assume that you are, in fact, a secret agent for some other bank or even the Post Office.

I shall not enter your doors again. I withdraw my account and enclose my cheque book which you may stuff where the monkey puts his nuts.

Yours fervently,

January 26 Received p.c. from bank: 'Your securities have been disposed of as directed.' I do not consider that funny.

January 27 Flamewell rang to ask what about that £300. He may well ask.

January 29 Today marks a turning point in my life. I shall never think ill of my daughter again. Gaye informed me this evening that *her* bank manager will lend us the money if I transfer my account there. I asked why he should lend money on the recommendation of a student when the efforts of a mature man had failed, and she said because he is a dirty old man and rather sweet on her.

I warned Gaye that I did not want her to do anything rash, but I would be most grateful if she would put in a word.

January 30 Flamewell suggests I have wall-lights fitted. He says he can do it for a few quid since the plaster has to be done anyway. Agreed.

January 31 Transferred my money to Barcloyds Bank. The manager is indeed an old man, but not obviously dirty. I tried to find out the exact relationship between him and my daughter but he merely said she was a sweet girl. He will grant me an overdraft of £200 for the time being.

Sent Flamewell a cheque for this sum, the balance to follow. Saw Askew in the evening, and he said why didn't I go to his bank, they always lend him money and never make any charges. Why is it that other people's banks, like other people's wives, are always so much more attractive than your own?

February 2 Gaye back at college. An ominous event occurred today. I had just rung Sheila to see if Flamewell had 'phoned, when the switchboard came through and asked if it was a private call.

In the afternooon I had to ring again but decided to make the call from a box in the street. Sir Phillip came in to ask for me and someone said I was telephoning in the street. Maureen says he put on that expression of maniacal cunning which we all dread so much.

February 3 Sir Phillip said today: 'I hope your horse won yesterday.' I suppose he is referring to my secret 'phone call. Later he came in and said, 'Where is the office *dark horse*?' Maureen burst into peals of feigned laughter. Contented myself with a mirthless smile.

February 6 A great day. Shei'a and I visited the new house and were astonished to see a great heap of rubble in the road outside. When we got inside we saw that Flamewell had started work!

He has already knocked out one of the interior walls downstairs which accounts for the heap of rubble. He has also destroyed the front garden wall, which is not supposed to come down. In fact he has wrought destruction all round, but at least things are moving. Went into the pub on the corner and it seemed much more pleasant than last time.

February 7 Rang Flamewell and was told he was busy on the conversion job in Broadwell Street, i.e. *our* house.

February 8 Flamewell suggests fitting an antique lamp over the front door. He says he can do it for almost nothing while the men are there. Agreed.

February 9 Called at Broadwell Street again this evening and was rather appalled at the amount of destruction which has gone on. Flamewell seems to have been carried away somewhat. I certainly did not ask him to tear down the front door and break all the windows downstairs. Neither was he supposed to pull down the wall of the small bedroom. I left a note pinned to the banisters asking him to destroy no more of my property without consulting me.

February 10 Rang Flamewell and asked him to explain why he has pulled down half the house. He apologised about the wall of the bedroom, but said it was only held up by thirteen layers of old wallpaper and it fell down as soon as they stripped it.

'Anyway,' he said, 'you'll find it easier to heat, having all one big room.'

He denied all knowledge of the front garden wall.

'It's that labourer of mine,' he said. 'Lazy isn't the word him. He'd knock a wall down sooner than lift anything over the top. You can't get good labour these days.'

He promised to speak severely to the man and to quote me for a new wall at a reduced price, although I fail to see why I should pay anything at all.

February 12 Today received an illiterate scrawl, apparently written with the butt end of a trowel, from Flamewell, asking for another £200. As Sir Phillip is visiting the Wolverhampton works I rang Maureen to tell her I would be late and went straight down to Broadwell Street.

I arrived at ten past nine, an hour at which I presume all good builders are normally at work, but the house was deserted. I waited half-an-hour and then went for a cup of tea at a café round the corner.

As I was leaving Flamewell entered, followed by a long-haired youth of about seventeen. I started to speak but the youth inserted sixpence in a juke box and began capering about in front of it. Conversation being impossible I conveyed to Flamewell by signs that I would see him at the house.

After threequarters of an hour the youth arrived and opened the front door by kicking it. I asked him where Flamewell was and he said he was playing the fruit machine in the café. I waited amid the wreckage, deafened by the youth's transistor, and when Flamewell arrived said, 'I am glad you have got here at last. I thought you builders were on the job at eight o'clock prompt.'

He winked cheerfully and replied, 'Touchy this morning, squire, aren't we? Did you bring the two hundred quid?'

'That is what I have come about,' I said sternly. 'Three weeks ago you had two hundred. What do you want another two hundred for?'

Flamewell said he had spent the original money and now wanted to buy bathroom fittings. I pointed out he had done nothing so far but demolish most of the house. He said: 'There's an eight-week delay in delivery on them fittings. If I cancel now you'll never get them.'

As I now realise that these days one's life is not one's own, but the property of ill-disposed people like bank managers and builders, I promised Flamewell a cheque and left, tearing my trousers on a nail. Larry, the labourer, said he tore his hair on the same nail yesterday.

February 14 Askew says if I want to impress the neighbours I should build a swimming pool. I said I couldn't afford it and he replied, 'Oh, you don't have to build it. Just put up the diving-boards first, and say you're waiting for the excavators.'

February 15 Sneaked out of office and went to Gaye's bank (which is, of course, mine now) and asked to see the manager. To my surprise it was a totally different person from the old man who lusted after my daughter. I asked where he was and got the reply, 'He retired last week.'

The new manager is much younger. I explained my errand and he said that far from lending me any more money he would be glad if I would reduce the original overdraft as quickly as possible! No doubt he wants to lend my money to some rickety commercial enterprise.

I spoke to one of the clerks and he confided that the previous manager had become a little strange in his old age.

'He started lending money to everyone,' said the clerk, tapping his forehead. 'I believe he took an early retirement at the request of head office.'

There is nothing I can do about it. I cannot keep chasing round London looking for a kind-hearted bank manager.

February 16 We have decided to sell the car. It is a three-year-old Austin 1100 and should fetch £400. This will relieve the immediate financial worry.

February 17 A thought has occurred to me: why doesn't Flamewell borrow the money for the building materials? He is just the sort of feckless tradesman they would lend it to. Why does the customer have to do all the worrying? Must stop thinking like this. That way madness lies.

February 18 Drove the car to Jackson's garage to see how much they would give for it, but it broke down on the way. I had to have it towed to Jackson's where they said the coil had worn out.

February 19 Played golf with Askew. He said why didn't I come to him, he knows where to lay his hands on £200 or £2,000 whenever he wants it. I notice Askew always makes these offers twenty-four hours too late.

February 20 Sent Flamewell cheque for £25 from current account and Sheila's wages. Perhaps he can buy a few nails with it.

February 22 Visited Broadwell Street. The heap of rubble outside is now 10 feet high. I hope they will remove it. Flamewell's lust for destruction seems to have been partially appeased and little more has been demolished.

While we were prowling around discussing decorations we heard a faint tapping on the wall. It came from next door. We paid no attention but when it kept on Sheila said we should go and see if they wanted anything.

We went outside into the inevitable rain and knocked. We heard a stick tapping down the passage and there was a terrible clanging of chains and an old woman opened the door six inches.

I said to her, 'Are you all right, madam? We heard you tapping on the wall.'

She made no reply but opened the door and by gestures invited us to follow her down the passage to the kitchen at the back and sat down in an old chair.

I then realised that the kitchen was three inches deep in water.

'Your men have torn my roof orf'

She waved her stick in the air and looking up I saw there was no roof, only some old canvas stretched across which had come away at one side and was letting in the rain.

'Your men have torn my roof orf,' the old woman explained.

She told us that the previous evening she was sitting in the kitchen with her cat when there was a great rending noise and Flamewell started to tear all the slates off the kitchen roof.

She screamed in alarm and Flamewell stuck his head through one of the holes and bellowed, 'It's all right, missus, we've got to do this to mend next door's roof.'

She sat there while the destruction went on, and then Larry the Labourer and Flamewell covered the hole with canvas. This blew away during the night since when it had rained continuously.

I put the canvas back in position and we mopped up most of the water. The old lady kept saying, 'They haven't got no right to go round tearing off people's roofs like that.' I assured her I would speak most severely to the wretched Flamewell.

We were puzzled by the fact that as fast as we mopped up the water, more poured in under the kitchen door. Then I went outside and found it was coming from a leaking downpipe on our house which Flamewell had deliberately bent so it would discharge in the old lady's yard.

I feel we have made a bad start with our neighbours.

Six

February 23 Rang Flamewell and commanded him to stop demolishing the house next door as well as our own. He expressed no concern, merely indignation that I should think badly of him.

'I bent that downpipe on your behalf,' he said plaintively. 'After all you don't want it leaking all over your yard.'

It is impossible to argue with him—his thought-processes are alien to those of a civilised creature. However, he said he would get Larry to look at it.

'Perhaps he can stop the leak with his hair,' I said.

February 24 Retrieved car from Jackson's. I do not like to sell it there, as they repaired it, so I took it to East Middlesex Motors. A man came out and kicked it and offered me £180. Drove away.

February 25 The Brentford and Chiswick Automobile Co. have offered me £160 for the car. They had a similar model for sale in the window at £400. Is this country of ours entirely occupied by thieves masquerading as builders, bankers, solicitors and car dealers?

February 26 Sheila and I took poor old Mrs. Wainwright in Broadwell Street some flowers this evening. I am pleased that she is in the dry again. Flamewell has put back her roof, having repaired the brickwork on my side.

Mrs. Wainwright says Flamewell has offered to repair her garden wall for nothing. I did not mention I was paying. She says she thinks Mr. Flamewell is a very nice man and it was a pity he was *ordered to take off her roof*.

February 27 Felt unusually happy today. No one is bothering me about anything.

February 28 Sold car to West Circular Carburettor Co. They gave me £185. The man said, 'There isn't any demand for this model, sir.'

March 1 Flamewell suggests that we have a built-in cupboard in the bedroom. As usual, he says he can do it for almost nothing while the chippies are there anyway. Agreed, with trepidation.

March 2 Sent £175 to Flamewell. It is like pouring money into an open drain.

March 3 Visited Broadwell Street (by bus). I miss the car. I kept changing gear and pressing imaginary pedals on the top deck. It's funny to think when I was courting Sheila we used to get the 65 to Richmond for an afternoon out and be as happy as larks.

Uncle Walter says money corrupts but I seem to be in the unfortunate position of being corrupted without having any money.

March 4 When I visited Broadwell Street today Larry the Labourer said to me, 'Do you know anything about this?'

He showed me a trench two feet wide and three feet deep which had been dug across the front garden. Of course I knew nothing about it. Larry said Flamewell doesn't know either. It is all very mysterious.

March 5 Passing the West Circular Carburettor Co. today I saw my car for sale as Bargain of the Week at £400. This represents £215 profit for the dealer who has probably done no more than polish it. I have no doubt the bank would fall over themselves to lend *him* money.

March 6 While trying to visit the house I was ejected from the bus for tendering the conductor a five-pound note. Had to buy a drink I didn't want to get change.

March 10 Letter received from bank manager asking when I will reduce my overdraft 'as the situation has changed since you entered into an arrangement with my predecessor'. This flagrant violation of their agreement so annoyed me that I wrote back in extremely violent terms.

After posting the letter I calmed down and wished I could retrieve the letter. I hung about the pillar-box until the postman came and said I had posted a letter by mistake and could he give it back to me? He said I would have to go to the sorting office and pay an interception fee. I went to The Crown instead.

March 11 Britain's monthly trade deficit was £76,000,000 last month. I could tell them why. The country's economy is in the hands of people like Flamewell and Atkins and the new bank manager.

March 12 No reply from bank manager. Hope letter got lost in the post.

March 13 No reply from bank manager. Sheila and I have talked over the money problem and decided that I must ask for a rise in salary. I have not had one for three years, not since Sir Phillip's photograph appeared in *The Condenser* upside down.

March 14 No reply from bank manager. Spent evening preparing and rehearsing a little speech for Sir Phillip when asking for a rise. Sheila, who is a member of the Operatic and Dramatic Society, said I was hamming it.

Later, in The Crown, I told Askew that I was worried

about my letter to the bank manager. He said there is no need to worry as long as I owe them money. While banks have no time for people with money in their account, they treat overdraft customers with every respect. It is nice to know.

March 15 Saw Sir Phillip today and asked for an increase in salary. He took the opportunity of giving me a long sermon on the need for thrift and economy.

'I bought my own house in 1944 when I was earning £11 a week,' he said.

I pointed out that in 1944 I had been earning a guinea a week as a private soldier, less a shilling deduction for haircut and barrackroom damages. A glazed expression came over his face and he replied, 'I am glad you agree with me.' I suppose that is a typical boardroom tactic. He said he would consider the matter and then left in a taxi for lunch at the Hilton.

March 16 Gaye wrote from college to say her grant has run out. For once I was able to decline to help her with a perfectly clear conscience.

March 18 Have been anxious to get a completion date from Flamewell but I cannot get hold of him, so I called in at Broadwell Street on the way to work. He was in the café round the corner, enjoying a simple snack of baked beans, sausages, bacon, egg, chips, tomatoes and fried bread. I asked when he expected to finish the job and he said there was a good chance of completing the building work in three weeks. The plumbing and electrical work should not take long.

I asked Flamewell about the trench in the garden and he said he thought I must have dug it. I said no, I thought *he* dug it.

'Strange things happen in the building trade, squire,' said Flamewell. 'I should leave it and see what happens.'

Got to the office at ten-thirty and tried to make it look as if I had come from the printers, holding a parcel of proofs ostentatiously. Nobby, the commissionaire, spoiled my entrance by saying Sir Phillip had been looking for me all morning.

When I saw Sir Phillip he said he was not happy about the last issue of *The Condenser*. He complained that the fitter featured on Page Three under the headline 'Employee Wins Top Pigeon Award' had caused the recent strike.

'I will not have paid agitators featured in my newspaper,' said Sir Phillip. 'Not even if they win twenty pigeon awards.'

March 20 Sheila and I visit the house this evening. Some progress has been made. The kitchen at the back has been rebuilt, and the bathroom is complete except for the plastering and plumbing. But we were very disturbed by a strange note which had been pushed through the letter-box. This read:

> Sir,
>
> If you do not have that heap of rubbish outside moved at once I shall tell the Council and they will send a man round and he will persecute you as it is a menace to health and children and to my son's motor-cycle which has no free access and they should do something about it.

It was unsigned. Presumably it came from a neighbour, but not old Mrs. Wainwright as she now thinks Flamewell is the nicest man on earth, and supplies him with endless cups of tea. She little realises he would divert the main sewer into her bedroom if it suited him.

However, I must admit the heap in the road *is* rather large, having now reached a height of about fifteen feet at the apex, which is crowned with a chamber pot. I am sure that did not come from our house. I left a note pinned on the banister asking Flamewell to remove the rubbish.

March 23 Rubbish not removed. But another trench has appeared, this time in the back garden. Who is the mystery trench-digger?

March 24 Sheila has left XYZ Electronics because she cannot work her new electric typewriter. I suppose that is

Astounded to find two workmen bricking up the front door

the penalty of going back to work after twenty years away. Sheila says it has a life of its own and it keeps jumping about. The carriage shot off the other day.

XYZ Electronics are so efficient they would not let her use her old machine which they took away.

March 25 Gaye wrote from college to say she had just failed an important exam and she believes the whole structure of University examinations needs overhauling. I can well believe it.

March 26 Received pay slip. I have been granted a rise of £75 a year (gross). I do not know if this is Sir Phillip's idea of a joke or a subtle hint to get rid of me. But the money will be useful for the house. It might just as well be paid direct to Flamewell.

March 27 Went to work late owing to dental appointment. Took the chance to visit Broadwell Street where I was astounded to find two workmen bricking up the front door! After examining the house to make sure it was the right one, I asked them to stop, pointing out that it was the back door that is to be altered.

To my astonishment they refused. They said they were hired by Flamewell and only he could tell them what to do. As I could not contact Flamewell, I plastered the house with messages and sent him the following telegram:

DEMAND INSIST YOUR MEN TO STOP BRICKING UP FRONT DOOR SPEEDLIEST IMPERATIVE URGENT.

March 28 At last ran Flamewell to earth. He thought it was a great joke about the front door.

'Funniest thing I've heard in years,' he said. 'I bet you nearly had a heart attack.'

He added genially, 'Don't worry, squire, *it won't add much to the bill*. I'll take care of you.'

March 30 Uncle Walter came to Broadwell Street with

me. We had to climb in the window as the front door has not yet been unbricked.

'There was a lot of rubbish built about this time,' said Uncle Walter. 'Unseasoned timber you've got there for a start, my boy. Riddled with worm no doubt. It was the age of the get-rich-quick Victorian speculative builder employing half-starved uneducated labour. Poor chaps were too hungry to lay a brick straight. If they weren't hungry they were drunk. You read *The Ragged-Trousered Philanthropists*, my boy, that'll tell you all about it. I tell you what, this house is damp. When you've got rheumatism like I have you can smell it a mile off.'

Incidentally Flamewell still has not removed the rubbish heap. Uncle Walter says rats will get in it and I shall be sent to gaol.

Against my advice he insisted on going into The Spread Eagle. As usual the landlord was in the other bar. I warned Uncle Walter not to offend him but he said, 'Nonsense, you don't know how to handle these people,' and began banging loudly on the counter and calling out, 'I say, do you mind, can we have some service please?'

The landord ignored this for some time and then came storming into the saloon bar and said to Uncle Walter, 'Why don't you —— off?'

'I beg your pardon,' said Uncle Walter, so he repeated his remark.

I led him outside and took him to The Crown.

'I don't know why you want to move to that unpleasant district,' said Uncle Walter.

March 31 Sheila has got a job with Knock Out Cough Drops Ltd. They are on the Great West Road. She is allowed a free tin of cough drops each week.

April 2 I believe Flamewell is using slave labour. When I visited Broadwell Street I found a little West Indian boy vainly trying to lift a wheelbarrow full of cement. He was alone on the premises. He says his name is Whitbread and he comes along after school.

I suggested that he took one handle of the wheelbarrow and I took the other. Unfortunately Whitbread seized his side with such ferocity that the whole load overbalanced and slid over my foot. It was like being in a plaster cast.

April 3 Gaye home from college. She brought with her a tall youth with a beard who is her boy friend. I have been unable to find out his name as he just mumbles when he speaks. I offered him a drink and he asked for Pernod. He spends all the time staring at the floor and clicking his fingers and jerking. Gaye says he is going to get a job with I.C.I. when he graduates, as he feels this will give him an opportunity for industrial sabotage on a spectacular scale.

Thinking to humour the lad (whom I took to be a Communist) I said agreeably, 'Well you've got to admit the Russians have a lot to their credit.'

He snarled 'Trotsky scum' and walked out of the room. Gaye says I have upset him and he will not come to the house again. We must be thankful for small mercies.

April 5 Flamewell says he has filled in the mysterious trenches and for good measure has removed the rubbish heap from outside the house.

Asked Flamewell about young Whitbread, and wasn't he rather young to be lifting heavy weights? Flamewell said he is teaching him the business. A likely tale.

April 6 As the weather is nice I bought myself a new No. 4 iron, a golf club I have needed for some time. I did not tell Sheila, as we have agreed to give up luxuries to pay for the house.

April 8 I am convinced women have a mysterious instinct which enables them to seek out trouble. Sheila has discovered my new golf club. She said she was dusting my clubs (a palpable lie) and she happened to count them and noticed there was one more. A typical woman's ploy. Sheila says if I can spend our money on golf clubs for myself then she will spend it on something for herself.

April 9 Sheila has bought an outrageous new hat. It looks like a weather vane. It is supremely useless and she admits it is not suitable for wearing out of doors. She says it is no more useless than my 4 iron, which is nonsense, as one often needs a 4 iron to clear the water hazard at the third hole. I tried to explain why I could not use another club but she would not listen.

April 11 Have discovered that Gaye's boy friend, who lives in Acton, is called Hugo. He gave her a record by some American, who apparently plays on bed-springs, entitled 'Money is a Dirty Word'. Gaye played it all evening and then asked me to give her ten shillings. When I objected she said my generation is obsessed with money.

April 12 Went to the cricket club annual dinner—first time for three years. Met old Sid Warner. He says why didn't I come to him, he knew a builder who would have fixed my house in no time. Also met young Jerry Sanders. He says why didn't I come to him, he knows a bank which lends any amount of money. The world is full of Askews.

April 13 At the office today they held the annual conference of executive staff at which lots of people come up from the foundry at Wolverhampton, and the other works. The routine is that during the morning everyone talks a load of hot air, we then get squiffy during a buffet lunch and talk hot air during the afternoon. Anyone expressing a genuine opinion soon finds himself out on his neck.

In the evening there was a dinner at a West End hotel. I am never happy in luxury hotels—it is all those servants creeping around, calling you 'sir' and secretly hating your guts. It cost two shillings to use the toilet. As soon as I entered an attendant filled a bowl full of water and laid a towel by it so I had to wash my hands and give him something.

The third time I went into the street and used a public convenience. At least they are free.

April 14 Second day of conference. Sir Phillip's big moment. In the morning he usually addresses the meeting for two hours on the necessity for pulling together, teamwork, etc. Questions are not allowed but the Production Manager makes a fulsome vote of thanks.

After Sir Phillip had been in progress for about an hour the 'phone by his elbow rang. He ignored it for as long as he could but eventually had to break off in the middle of an appeal for economy to answer.

A terrible squawking noise came from it, as if someone was bellowing at the top of his voice, and Sir Phillip went very pale and put the receiver down. He then said in that grave-like tone he uses when he is furious, 'Does anyone here know a person called Flamewell?'

I said yes, I did, and Sir Phillip said, 'He asked me to say that your roof has just fallen in.'

Seven

April 15 Unable to continue diary owing to emotional stress.

April 16 I can now fill in the details of the Disaster in Broadwell Street. According to Flamewell the roof collapsed when he removed part of the staircase. I said that I couldn't see the connection unless the staircase was supporting the roof and he said yes, it did seem queer, but he reckoned somehow the roof and the stairs must be connected.

'Strange things happen in these old houses, squire,' he told me. I agreed.

Flamewell says he will make out an estimate for repairing the roof. Meanwhile I shall inspect the damage. I have not yet been able to bring myself to do so.

April 17 Sheila says, didn't the surveyor say anything about the roof? I now remember that he was too fat to get up there, and contented himself with flashing a torch in from afar.

In p.m. I contacted Askew, and told him what his surveyor friend had done and asked if I could sue him. Askew says I might be able to, but he has heard that the poor chap is in a nursing home.

'If you really feel like sueing him I should go ahead,' said Askew, 'he's too far gone to put up any defence.'

Sheila says of course I cannot sue the surveyor, she would never forgive herself, poor chap, gibbering and salivating in a nursing home, etc., etc. Nobody seems to think about me gibbering and salivating in a mental home, a fact which is strongly on the cards. Am I becoming an alcoholic? Tonight I drank half a bottle of whisky without any effect whatsoever.

April 18 Forced myself to visit house. I had imagined it would look as if a bomb had hit it, but in fact the roof is still there, it just looks all sort of wavy, as in an old Elizabethan cottage.

While I was standing outside the house looking at it, it gave a sort of creak and sagged a little more, and three slates fell off. I stepped back in alarm and noticed faces peering from every window.

April 19 Flamewell says he can repair roof for £80. He will jack up the joists or corble them or something. He has talked to a roofing expert. However, if scaffolding is needed it will cost £150 just to put it up.

April 20 Sir Phillip met me in the corridor today and said he hoped that in future I would not have the executive conference interrupted by personal 'phone calls from relatives. He stalked off in a temper before I could explain.

April 24 Gaye says that Hugo her boy friend says the new house ought to be used as a shelter for drug addicts. I hope Gaye is not starting to take drugs. While she was reading this evening I peered closely at her face to see if her pupils had shrunk to pinpoints and she said, 'Why are you staring at me maniacally, Daddy?' I said she reminded me of her mother.

April 25 The dreaded Flamewell telephoned. To my surprise he said they had fixed the roof! I was delighted. Unfortunately he spoiled my pleasure by adding that they had dropped some jacking machinery through the bedroom ceiling.

Flamewell also asks me to give a bonus to Larry the

Labourer, who apparently nearly sacrificed his life, sliding down the slates and preserving himself by hanging on to the guttering. The guttering was wrecked and will cost £15 to replace.

'We were trying to save you paying for scaffolding,' said Flamewell in an injured tone. 'The things we do for you, squire.'

April 26 Am rather worried about the number of men around the house. I hope Flamewell is not over-indulging himself on my money. Taking advantage of a business call I went to Broadwell Street and was alarmed to find seventeen men there.

To make matters worse, none of them were doing any work. They were all sitting around reading the *Daily Mirror*. However, they nodded pleasantly at me when I arrived and went on reading.

One of the carpenters said, 'This is a nice house you've got here, sir.' He made a sort of bed for himself out of a pile of shavings and was lying down drinking tea.

I asked Flamewell in a whisper if he really needed all these men and he boomed out all over the house, 'What do you think, Charlie, the guvnor thinks we've got too many men on the job.'

Charlie said you needed them on a job like this, he'd never seen woodwork in such a state. It was all most embarrassing so I did not press the point.

April 27 Gaye went up to the house with her mother. They say it is still full of men in aprons reading the *Daily Mirror*. Sheila says that the appearance of Gaye, who like most young women today habitually goes around half-naked, brought forth a slight stir of interest. Gaye announces she is going to a rave with Larry the Labourer.

I merely remarked that I hoped he would not trip over his hair and she rushed out of the room slamming the door.

April 28 If anybody else asks, 'How is your new house coming along?' I shall scream. I believe I must have been

Nodded pleasantly at me

asked that question seven hundred and fifty times in the last year. Today six people asked me. They do not want an answer, they interrupt before you have finished speaking and start telling of their own experiences.

April 29 Had to visit Wolverhampton works yesterday, so on returning today I went up to the house instead of going to the office. It is positively swarming with men. Flamewell said the chippies are here and the plumbers. He asked me to mark where I wanted the electric power points. I really feel we are getting somewhere at last.

April 30 Askew says I should not visit the house so often. But there is no knowing what Flamewell will do unless I keep an eye on things.

May 1 Some of the army of men have left the house, leaving behind about fifty *Daily Mirrors* and one copy of the *Sun*. While inspecting the work I noticed something odd about the bathroom. This is an old bedroom which we have had converted, and as it is a big room we are having a shower fitted at one end as well as a bath.

The shower has been fitted in one corner as agreed, but they have put the tiles in the other corner! I could hardly believe my eyes so I examined the fittings carefully, and there is no doubt that one corner of the room has been tastefully tiled in blue, with plastic curtains round the corner, while on the other side of the room there is a shower spray jutting out from a bare wall.

I cannot decide whether I am mad or the builders.

May 2 Flamewell being absent I managed to find the plumber who assured me he fitted the shower spray exactly where instructed. I then found the tiler who also assured me that he put the tiles exactly where marked.

I pointed out that it hardly mattered where the shower was as long as the water coincided with the tiles and asked if they could get together. The plumber said he wasn't moving no pipes. The tiler said he wasn't moving no tiles. I pleaded for half an hour with no result.

May 3 Phoned Flamewell. He was out but I left a message asking him to look at the shower urgently. The man in the office asked, 'How do you spell shower?' This is the sort of thing which does not inspire confidence.

May 4 Monthly trade statistics bad again. No surprise to me. I must ask Flamewell if he has ever been in the export business.

May 6 Sir Phillip called me into his office and asked if I was all right. I said it was the house and he replied, 'Haven't you moved in *yet*? You fellows don't know how to organise things.'

He was never nearer death.

May 8 Flamewell rang and said it was all right, he had fixed the business about the plumber and the tiler.

'That sort of thing requires tact if I may say so, squire,' he confided. 'You've got to have the knack of handling labour. It's no use going at it like a bull at a gate.'

May 10 Sheila called in at Broadwell Street after work this evening to take some measurements for curtains and came home with an alarming story, namely that the shower spray and the tiles have *both* been moved. The shower is now half-way between each corner.

I phoned Flamewell at his home and he said yes, this was the solution they had agreed on.

'You can't expect a craftsman to back down,' he said. 'They have their pride, the same as you.'

He added that the alteration will cost me £50.

May 12 I am not a religious man, but I am becoming more and more convinced that the Catholics have a good deal on their side. There must be some supernatural plan behind our sufferings.

May 13 Shall not visit house again until it is finished. Every time I go I become distressed. I find I am breathing hard all the time. Sheila says it is blood pressure. My mother had an uncle who died of blood pressure, but not until he was 85.

May 14 Forced to visit house today despite my resolution, as Flamewell wants to know if I really want the electric meters on the bedroom wall. I do not, I distinctly told him I wanted them under the stairs, but he says well they have appeared in the bedroom anyway. I know who is going to pay for moving them.

May 15 Considering I swore never to visit the house again I seem to be constantly going there. This evening I went to pick up my cigarette lighter, which I left behind yesterday.

It is fortunate I did so, for just as I was walking down the road there was a loud explosion and to my horror I saw a dense cloud of smoke rising up behind the house. It was like the time in the war when Dinger Bell bet me ten bob he could drop a lighted cigarette in the petrol tank without anything happening.

On running back inside I found a man who had been putting up shelves in the kitchen leaning weakly against the draining-board. He had no eyebrows and was covered in filth. The entire kitchen was black.

I led the man into the garden where after a rest and a cigarette he recovered a little. As soon as he regained his strength he turned on me with a torrent of abuse. It appears that the explosion was caused by the glue used to stick Formica on the shelves, as this gives off an inflammable vapour.

Halfway through his work he realised that the gas pilot light in the Ascot was alight, but even as he moved to turn it off he was enveloped in a sheet of flame. If he could find who lit the pilot light he would first kill them and then sue them.

I thought it better to say nothing, and took him to hospital where they said there was nothing wrong that a good bath and time wouldn't cure.

May 16 Flamewell says the kitchen will have to be repainted, and this will add £25 to the bill, as if I didn't know. I said whoever lit the pilot light should pay.

May 17 Abusive phone call received from unknown woman. I was forced to hang up.

May 18 Further abusive call received.

May 19 No abusive call today.

May 20 Abusive call. This time I did not put down the 'phone but asked politely, 'Madam, will you kindly state your business?' After a good deal of further insult it turned out she was the wife of the injured carpenter and she wanted to know what compensation I was going to pay for the loss of her husband and breadwinner.

When I said he was not seriously hurt she shouted, 'Hurt? Not hurt? He can hardly walk to the doctor for his sick note. He sits at home all day trembling, hardly able to lift a cup of tea to his lips. And you say he's not hurt?'

I refrained from saying that as far as I could see he only used to sit down all day at my house, although he seemed to find no difficulty in holding a cup of tea to his lips. I decided it was time Atkins earned his money and asked her to contact him.

May 21 Flamewell wrote to inform me solemnly that according to the sworn testimony of Larry the Labourer I had been seen to light the pilot light of the gas and therefore I would be held responsible for paying for the repainting of the kitchen. I knew I would have to pay in the end but I will never admit to igniting the gas, since I have never been near the Ascot.

Rang up Flamewell and told him as much and he replied, 'It is not for me to doubt anybody's word, squire. It is true that seven men have sworn they saw you light that gas but you are entitled to your story. If you are willing to pay for the damage then I am happy to forget the whole matter, as far as I can.'

These are the straits that buying a house reduces you to. If anyone had spoken to me like that two years ago I would have told him to take a running jump at himself.

May 22 Sir Phillip called me in to complain that last month's *Condenser* was late coming out. Of course it was. I could have produced five *Condensers* in the time spent on the house. However, I took the opportunity to say I needed an assistant.

To my surprise Sir Phillip agreed. I think he wants to train someone to take my place. I do not entirely blame Sir Phillip. If I treated him with half the servility I treat Flamewell and the bank manager I would be on the board by now.

May 24 What has gone wrong? The house is deserted. Even Larry the Labourer has vanished. But everything seems nearly finished now, except for the decorating, the central heating and one or two small jobs.

May 25 Flamewell wants another £150. There is nothing for it but to sell my life insurance policy, which is only five years old and worth about £200 surrender value. Thus in eighteen short months I have lost my pension, my savings, my provision for old age, and very nearly my job. In exchange I have a mortgage and a house not yet ready to live in.

May 27 Sheila and I checked the work on the house thoroughly. The electric meter has now been put in the airing cupboard, not under the stairs. This is probably because the door of the cupboard under the stairs has been fitted to open inwards so it is impossible even to get in.

There are dozens of other irritating things wrong. To start with, the shower spray has been fitted so it throws water over the ceiling. I cannot understand the mentality of a person who would fit a shower spray upside down.

The bath taps are of different sizes—an ordinary one and a tiny little one, like a doll's tap. Hot water comes from the cold tap and cold from the hot tap. The plug is too small for the hole. However, this doesn't matter as the chain is too short and it doesn't reach anyway.

The only signs of the wall-lamps which Flamewell suggested are bare wires sprouting all over the house. The antique lamp over the front door (another of Flamewell's suggestions) is not connected to anything. An entire floorboard is missing in the front bedroom. I made a list of jobs which needed doing and intend to give it to Flamewell.

May 29 Cannot contact Flamewell. He has vanished. There is no answer to my calls.

June 2 Still no sign of Flamewell. Posted list of jobs and asked him to contact me.

June 3 Wrote to GPO about having telephone installed.

June 5 Sheila and I went up to Wolverhampton for the annual cricket match, head office *v.* works. Sir Phillip, who is very keen on cricket, attaches great importance to this. He always plays and all the bowlers deliberately bowl slow long hops outside his off stump.

Unfortunately I was still batting when he came to the wicket. The first ball was the traditional long hop but Sir Phillip was so dazed with age and gin that he missed it altogether and it stuck in the top of the wicket-keeper's pad. To my horror he looked wildly round and called for a run. I sent him back but he was run out by yards. He would not speak to me for the rest of the day.

Sheila said surely no man would be so childish as to go into a huff because he was run out but I said that is just how the average male mind works.

June 7 Printed acknowledgment received from GPO re 'phone. No trace of Flamewell.

June 9 Passed Sir Phillip in the corridor. He snarled at me: 'That run was my call, you know.'

June 10 Leaving word with Nobby and Maureen that I had gone to the printers, I sneaked down to Broadwell Street during the day hoping to catch Flamewell but he was nowhere to be seen. I went into the garden when an astonishing thing happened: I could have sworn that I saw Flamewell's face appear on top of the roof of a house in the street at the back. It peered evilly over the top of the roof and remained there for a minute before disappearing.

Can it be that the terrible events of the past few months have attacked my sanity?

June 11 No news of Flamewell. Not having heard from GPO rang telephone manager's office but the number was engaged.

June 12 Glad to say not going mad. Sheila was down at the house today measuring up again and she says she distinctly saw Flamewell *standing on a chimney stack in the next street.* Ought I to contact the police? If he has had a brainstorm and is leaping around local roofs like a sort of Phantom of the Rue Morgue he should be apprehended for his own good.

June 14 No news from GPO or Flamewell. Not allowed to speak to telephone manager but his office told me to ask engineers about the progress of my application for a 'phone. Engineers engaged.

June 17 Called at house and almost fainted with horror. There is a great conical mound of solid concrete 6 ft high blocking the front path. Rushed in to Mrs. Wainwright and asked if she knew anything about it and she said yes, a load of ready-mixed concrete came this morning and they couldn't find anyone there so they just poured it all out.

I am beside myself. It is all Flamewell's fault—he obviously ordered the stuff weeks ago. There is hardly room for the postman to get by.

June 19 While searching for Flamewell (unsuccessfully)

dropped in at The Spread Eagle. The man in the corner says he believes an old right of way goes through my house. He says the only way to stop a right of way is to have an Act passed in Parliament. The mind boggles at the thought of Atkins getting his teeth into that one.

June 21 Got through to telephone engineers, who managed to convey the impression they were doing a great favour by even speaking to me.

'The trouble is, sir,' said a voice, 'that everyone these days wants everything done in a hurry.'

I pointed out that so far I had waited three weeks and no one had even had the courtesy to write and tell me there would be a delay. I asked him when the job would be done.

The voice said it was impossible to say. A new line has to be laid from the manhole in the pavement to the house (distance—six feet), and this task is at present beyond the resources of the Post Office. I was about to make some spirited rejoinder when there was a noise like a telephone exchange in pain and the line went dead.

June 23 No news of Flamewell. There was a letter at the house asking me to ring the Water Board.

June 24 Rang Water Board. They wanted to know what I meant *by filling in their trenches dug six months ago*. They reserve the right to charge me if they have to dig them again. I said they might have warned me about the trenches and they replied they put a card through the door. I must have burned it along with soap powder ads.

Eight

June 25 The mystery of Flamewell is solved. While Sheila and I were at Broadwell Street, making endless plans as usual, there was a knock at the door (the bell does not work because the man who fitted it did not bother to drill a hole for the wires). I opened it and a man asked if Mr. Flamewell was there.

We said no, and he said could he leave a message? Please to ask Mr. Flamewell to come tomorrow.

I said, 'Come where?' He replied, 'To my house. He has been working on my roof for three weeks.'

I questioned the man carefully and he said Flamewell was doing jobs all round the district and using my house as his headquarters.

'He is doing my roof, an extension to Mrs. Smith's kitchen and Mr. Brown's garden wall,' said the man. 'He seems a very efficient, obliging sort of chap.'

No wonder no further progress has been made on the house!

I told the man I would not give Flamewell a message but he could give Flamewell a message from me, i.e. '. . . off.' The man left, giving me a peculiar look.

June 26 Wrote to Flamewell today and told him I would not settle his account unless he finished off the odds and ends such as wires sticking out of walls, doors off hinges, etc., etc. I would not require him to finish the decorating as we think it would be quicker to do that ourselves. The main thing is to get Flamewell out and get ourselves *in.*

Also asked what he intended to do about the mound of solid concrete which sits leering in the middle of the front garden.

June 27 Wrote to telephone manager explaining that this is the twentieth century.

June 28 Much to my surprise I received Flamewell's final account today. It is quite obvious he has just thought up the first figure that came into his head and doubled it. The total bill is £450 more than the estimate and this does not include decorating. All the little extra jobs which he persuaded me he could do cheaply, such as the built-in wardrobe, have been charged at treble the estimated cost. So has the roof repair.

The account is also couched in the vaguest possible terms, e.g. 'to scraping out, corbling and making good . . . £215 8s 6d'. How can an ordinary citizen translate this sort of thing?

Along with the bill was a scribbled note: 'Sorry re delay, if you go round you will find all completed. Regret estimate exceeded slightly, but you ordered a lot of extra work.'

June 30 Went round and inspected Flamework's handiwork. There is still no sign of him but an attempt has been made to finish off. At first sight all looked in order, but when I switched on one of the wall-lights downstairs, it fell off the wall. Bell still not connected. The kitchen door, which was missing, has been replaced with one screw in each hinge, so it fell off as I opened it. Heaven knows what other disasters lie hidden.

A few feeble hacks have been made at the concrete heap, after which they had obviously given up in disgust.

July 1 Printed p.c. received from telephone manager saying the contents of my letter have been noted.

July 2 The worm has turned. This evening I sat down with half a bottle of Scotch and wrote to Flamewell saying that he had already had several hundred pounds from me, and I would pay the rest when I got the council grant and not before. I added that I would be deducting £100 from his bill for various shortcomings and he need not visit the property again unless it was to remove the cheese sandwiches and newspapers left by his men.

Felt quite revolutionary. Am convinced that one day the ordinary citizens of this country will rise up against their oppressors, i.e. builders, bank managers, plumbers, solicitors, telephone managers and so forth.

July 3 Awoke with a vile headache and feeling that perhaps my letter to Flamewell had not been wise.

July 4 (U.S. Independence Day): After three hours hacking vainly at the concrete mound in the front garden I have decided to grow Virginia Creeper all over it and leave it. We shall call it Flamewell's Folly. It doesn't really do much harm, except it blocks some of the light from the living-room window, and it will make things a bit difficult for delivery men. The milkman can leave the milk on top of it.

July 5 Need not have worried about my letter to Flamewell. Askew told me in The Crown tonight that builders always expect you to knock £100 from their bill, so they stick it on in advance. If I wanted to save £100 I should have knocked off £200. It is impossible to win. I deeply regret that I did not follow an adolescent desire to be a monk.

July 6 When I said to Sheila I felt like becoming a monk, she said the vow of chastity shouldn't worry me at my age and I should manage the vow of poverty without much difficulty as well.

July 7 Day of decision. We shall move early in September whatever happens. Our first task must be to find new tenants for the flat.

July 8 Advertised flat, rang removal people for estimate, and wrote to Town Hall asking if I could now have the grant.

July 10 Borrowed a spade from Askew and went to attack the garden of the new house. Flamewell's baleful influence, like that of some evil genie, still remains however. As I was digging over a flower-bed I came across the most incredible load of rubbish, rusty springs, kettles, tin cans, broken glass, plaster, planks and heaven knows what else.

I can only conclude that Flamewell has got rid of the rubbish heap outside in the road by burying it in the garden. The mystery is that all sorts of things like old kettles have sprouted which never came out of the house. It is as if they had grown, like plants. Luckily, one flower bed is still fairly clear and contains some flowers of different sorts (I must find out their names).

Watered them carefully from an old cup left behind by the builders. While I was doing so a large fat cat, which had been sitting on the garden wall watching me, jumped down on top of the flowers, destroyed several to clear a space, relieved itself, and then buried its little offering by digging a great pit.

As I was chasing the cat round the garden with my spade, a man in braces stuck his head over the wall and called me to stop.

'I shall have the law on you,' he shouted, 'torturing a harmless pussy like that. We've had enough trouble with you, what with your stinking heaps of rubbish outside in the road.'

He went away before I could reply, but for the rest of the evening I could hear his voice muttering 'Murderer' on the other side of the wall. Old Mrs. Wainwright says he has always been like this.

July 11 No news from GPO. Dug up old pram in garden.

July 12 When I got home from the office Sheila said, 'Thank heavens you're back, the 'phone has not stopped ringing for an hour with people wanting to see the flat. We have got five lots of them coming this evening.'

Raced through evening meal and ran round to the off-licence for a bottle of Scotch in case a drink would help clinch the deal. Sheila made a large pot of coffee, which she kept hot on the gas, together with some sandwiches, as we feel a warm welcome might make all the difference to letting the flat.

By nine o'clock no one had turned up and I asked Sheila if she was *sure* she had asked them to come tonight. She said she was not half-witted. At ten o'clock we decided to call it a day and ate all the sandwiches and drank the coffee. I am afraid I had already drunk most of the Scotch. Had terrible indigestion and did not sleep a wink all night.

July 13 While Sheila was washing her hair this evening I decided to cut my toenails in the living-room, as there was something I did not want to miss on the television. As I was doing so there was a prolonged ring at the door. I hobbled to it in my bare feet and outside were a man and a woman who said they had come about the flat. I had no choice but to ask them into the living-room, which was covered in toenail parings. It was most embarrassing.

The couple were very rude about everything. The man pulled aside our sideboard, revealing the damp patch on the wall it had been placed there to hide. Fortunately, on Askew's advice, I had removed the bulb from our worst room, the spare bedroom where the rain has got in around the window frame and the plaster is crumbling, and had blacked out the window, so when they came to inspect it I said I used it for photography. However, the man took out a torch and flashed it all over the bad patches by the window.

In the middle of all this Sheila burst out of the bathroom looking like something from an 'X' film and apologising profusely for being in the middle of washing her hair. The man said he would let us know.

July 14 A young man in a Jaguar and his girl friend called round this evening. Girl is looking for a flat, and Mummy and

Daddy are going to pay the rent. They said they liked the place but would Sheila be prepared to come back and clean for her once a week? With heavy sarcasm I said would they like me to come along and do a few odd jobs occasionally? The man said that would be a jolly good idea.

Sheila said we had someone else coming and would let them know.

July 15 We went round to Jack Askew's tonight. I said we were going to decorate the house ourselves and Askew said, 'Why don't you have a decorating party? Get in half a dozen friends and lay on some drinks and some food and you can finish off most of the painting in one day.' Sheila thought it was a great idea.

July 16 A couple of peculiar old spinsters called to see flat. They have an obsession about the floor collapsing, and both of them jumped up and down all over the lounge like a pair of vultures unable to settle. Mrs Goldsmith came up to complain. The spinsters say they could not feel *safe* on the third floor.

July 17 Askew says he will give us a moving-in present of a handpainted nameplate for the front gate (as usual, he knows a man). He offered me the following choice of names:

The Leekings
The Seekings
The Reekings
The Old Almshouse
The Old Rectory
The Old Mill

I said I didn't like any of those but Askew says you must give the house tone. I said he could choose the one he liked best and it would be a surprise for us.

July 18 Bought a small electric fire today and took it down Broadwell Street, so we shall have something to use for drying out the house after decorating. As soon as I switched it on there was a sheet of flame and it blew up, so I took it back to the shop.

The man in the shop said, 'The trouble today is that people expect things to last for ever.' I said it only lasted two seconds. 'If I wanted to buy a firework,' I added, 'I would not pay fourteen pounds for one.'

The man refused to replace the fire, but said they will send it back to the makers. It may be three weeks before we hear anything as the factory is on holiday. Why is it that the simplest thing is almost impossible in this country?

July 19 No news from GPO, but we have let the flat! They are a nice young couple who got married recently. Just a few formalities to complete. They will move the day after we leave so that will be one financial burden less.

July 20 Decorating party fixed for end of August, which will just give time for the place to dry out before we move. Sheila will invite some people from the Operatic Society. Then there will be Jack Askew and his wife, and Askew is bringing two chaps who used to play rugby for the Vipers with him.

July 21 The cat from next door has been at my flowers again. It is becoming insolent. It sat on the wall and looked at me and then solemnly proceeded to pad across the flower bed and do its fearful deed within easy reach of my lifted spade.

July 22 Forgot to mention that I left a key at the Town Hall for the building inspector to look round. I have now received a letter from him which fills me with dismay. He says the grant will be withheld 'until all the conditions are complied with'.

Immediately rang Town Hall, and after about half an hour being shunted from one department to another I was told that there is no outside ventilation in the kitchen food-store and until there is I cannot have *any* of the £312. So for want of an air-brick costing £5 to fit I am being penalised

£307. The Faceless Men are in control. It is like being back in the Army.

July 23 Spent day recklessly using the firm's telephone to ring fourteen builders, none of whom can insert a simple air-brick in under three months.

July 24 The curtains have come. Went down with Sheila to fit them this evening. It was rather a rough old job, as putting up curtain rails is not my strong point, and eventually I had to nail the dining-room curtains to the woodwork. However, they look very nice. Unlike the garden where that cat is at it again. The flower bed looks like a war-time strong point, all holes and bumps.

July 25 Askew says if you pour petrol on the flowers it keeps away cats.

July 26 Poured petrol on flowers. Bedroom curtain rail has collapsed.

July 27 Went stark, raving mad, am pleased to say. I borrowed a sledge hammer from Uncle Walter in Harrow, and smote a great hole in the kitchen wall behind the food cupboard. I then wrote to the building inspector and asked him to come and look at it.

July 28 Bank manager wrote unpleasant letter to me, reminding me that I had overdrawn by £35 (it was the curtains which did it). Sent back a cutting from the *Telegraph* about the bank granting a million pound overdraft to a trade union to help them strike. But these gestures are only the beating of tiny wings in the trap.

July 29 The complete silence of the GPO re my 'phone is worrying me. The telephone manager will not reply to my letters, except for a stupid printed postcard in acknowledgement. It is very difficult dealing with the Faceless Ones.

Went to the Oval after tea-interval and met Askew and George Burrows. Askew says the only way to attract attention from the GPO is either to assume high military rank or threaten to complain to an MP.

After getting home I wrote to the telephone manager stating that during the war I was at the head of 2,000 men. This was strictly true, because when the brigade moved from Wales to Scotland I was driving the leading lorry. It was the time when Chalky White drove down the adjutant. I signed the letter 'Cpl. Bull', making the word 'Cpl.' look like 'Col.'. Can do no more.

July 30 For the umpteenth time this year I sneaked away from work (leaving a message that I had neuralgia) and met the building inspector. Took him to see the great hole in the food store, through which the rain was blowing. He studied it for several moments and much to my surprise said, 'That is all right. The regulations say the food store has got to be ventilated—they don't say how.'

The food store certainly *is* ventilated, since there is a two-foot hole in the back of it through which dirt, dust, rain and fog can stream in. I shall fill up the hole when I have the grant.

The inspector regaled me with horror stories of grants not granted. 'There was one elderly couple,' he said, 'whose bathroom was six inches smaller all round than in the specification. I made them rebuild it.'

I said, 'You must have a happy life,' and he said yes, it was very enjoyable, you met all sorts of people.

July 31 My flowers have all turned black and died. They cannot like petrol. Unfortunately the cat appears to do so, and it has been playing happily amidst the wreckage. Must speak to Askew.

August 1 Went to gas showrooms today to buy a gas fire. Apparently this is impossible. I pointed out the model I wanted and they said it was not in stock. I said what about the one I was pointing at? They said it was for display only.

He studied it for several moments

I replied, what was the point of displaying a fire if it was not in stock?

However, as usual, it is like trying to argue with a demented person. In the end I chose a cheaper fire and I now have to wait for them to fit it.

August 2 Askew says he is sorry, it was not petrol but pepper that keeps cats off flowers.

August 3 Carpet people ready to fit carpets. We are having new ones downstairs and the old ones upstairs.

August 4 My letter to the Telephone Manager has worked! At the house this evening I found a printed card from the GPO saying they came to install 'phone but I was not in. Also card from Gas Board saying they came to fit fire, but I was not in. As they did not let me know they were coming I do not know what they expected to find.

August 5 Rang 'phone engineers, who were their usual charming selves. No, sir, we can never guarantee when we are coming. We thought you wanted a 'phone urgently, sir. In this job it's impossible to fix a time, sir. People are so odd, sir.

I asked if they expected me to wait in an empty house eight hours a day until it pleased them to arrive. They obviously did, but finally compromised by promising to come on Tuesday at an unspecified time. Gas Board cannot come on Tuesday but will come Monday, also at unspecified time.

August 6 I now have an assistant at work. His name is David. He is 23 and was a reporter on a weekly paper in South Wales. Sir Phillip called me in and said pointedly he now expects a very high standard from *The Condenser*.

I have had to confide in David that owing to the fact that this country is in the hands of insane persons, 90 per cent of my energies are directed towards the simple task of moving house, but as soon as possible I hope to be allowed to resume normal work. He says what can you expect in capitalist society. I think he may be rather revolutionary.

August 7 Gaye is back home. She vanished for a fortnight after leaving college. I wish she would stop going out with Hugo.

August 8 Am so angry can hardly hold pen. Arrived at house at 9.15 to await gas men, having lied away my soul all round the office. They did not arrive until quarter past twelve. They then dropped the fire on the floor and went.

I asked, 'Aren't you going to install it?' and they replied, 'No, guv, we are the deliverers. You will have to wait for a fitter to put it in.'

August 9 If I was angry yesterday, today I am beside myself. I arrived again at 9.15 and waited all day for the GPO, who never arrived. Did not even dare leave house for lunch, but hunger drove me out about three. Returned to find a card on the floor: *GPO called but no reply.*

August 10 Young David says Sir Phillip was in and out of my office all yesterday wanting to know where I was. Maureen says he wanted to see me before he went to Wolverhampton. He has gone away for several days, thank goodness. By a miracle I have arranged for the GPO and the gasmen to arrive on the same day next week.

August 11 The carpet people rang today urgently demanding to be allowed to lay the carpets. Commendable efficiency. Unfortunately I don't want the carpets laid until we can arrange the decorating party, so I asked them if they could wait a week or two. They said no, the layers would be going on holiday and the carpets must be *laid at once.*

August 12 Carpets fitted. Could not believe all would go well, and became convinced colours were wrong, and they were fitting stair carpet in dining-room and vice-versa. Became so neurotic I had to go to a call-box and ring Sheila at her work. The men must have thought I was mad.

While they were at work I did one or two jobs in the garden and threw a half-brick at the cat from next door. Fortunately there is still plenty of ammunition left. Dug up what appeared to be part of a 25-pounder gun. Can't think where it all comes from.

August 15 Maureen says Sir Phillip arrived from Wolverhampton yesterday afternoon and immediately asked for me. She told him I was at the printer's. Unfortunately David told Sir Phillip I was away with malaria. Meanwhile Nobby had told him I was entertaining an important visitor from overseas. Ah well, I have had a good run.

August 16 Arose at dawn to ensure I got to Broadwell Street early. Was able to give Sheila her breakfast before she caught the bus to the Great West Road. Arrived at the house about 8.15 and sat and smoked until 9.45 when the GPO arrived. They immediately erected a small tent over the pavement and dug a trench across the front garden, demolishing part of the fence. They said they had to connect up with the main cable. It would be a two-day job.

Gasmen arrived after lunch, but could not fit the fire as the backplate was wrong. They would come back next day, next week, or next year. I refuse to worry any more about that gas fire. It will come in its own good time and nothing I can do will hasten the Gas Board.

August 17 Dawn patrol for GPO as usual. Saw them at work and dashed to the office. Maureen says Sir Phillip asking for me since 9.15. I went in and he stared at me for a long time in silence, finally remarking, 'How kind of you to look in. I trust your malaria is better.'

I said I had been on retrospective holiday. Sir Phillip asked what the devil that was and I explained that I had taken time off for the house and had decided to knock a week off my holiday to compensate. Sir Phillip said he was deeply moved.

He wants me to mark the 25th anniversary of his taking office next month with a large photograph of himself on the front page with appropriate caption. I could do an appropriate caption in one word.

August 18 The 'phone is installed. True, it is in the wrong place, but it is there and it works. Unfortunately, they have only left one directory—L–R, and that is two years old. I rang Sheila and told her the 'phone was in. Then got her to ring back to make sure it works both ways.

August 19 Played golf with Uncle Walter. I have never played worse and no wonder. I don't see the ball, I see faces of gasmen, GPO men, carpet men and so forth. Uncle Walter says he always pretends my aunt's face is on the ball, as this improves his driving.

'It gives it that extra bite,' he said.

August 20 We gave ourselves a day off from the house and took a bus to Burnham Beeches, where we saw a snake. Sheila said it reminded her of Flamewell. I laughed so much I felt sick.

Nine

August 21 Maureen says her father has been waiting eight months for a telephone. He says I must have used influence to get one so quickly (i.e. in three months). It is the first time one of Askew's cracked ideas has worked.

August 22 Spent day getting ready for decorating party tomorrow. Luckily the council grant arrived by second post, although most of it is already mortgaged, including £50 I borrowed from Uncle Walter. Sheila says I must put at least £100 away in a special fund for emergencies. They will come soon enough the way Sir Phillip is looking at me.

Spent about £30 on paints, paintbrushes, rollers and so forth. Also another £10 on booze. Sheila bought a ham at Sainsbury's so I got some red wine. Gaye, who has been working as a waitress at an hotel in Salcombe, arrived unexpectedly in the afternoon.

I expressed surprise and she said, 'Surely you don't think I would stay away at a time like this?' I shall never understand that girl. Unfortunately she is bringing Hugo tomorrow. Told her his beard would come in useful for cleaning brushes.

August 23 Arrived at Broadwell Street about ten as we didn't want any of our guests to be hanging around outside.

I have not been outside on Sunday a.m. so early for years. It is quite pleasant.

The lace curtains were twitching busily. Called on old Mrs Wainwright and said she wasn't to worry if she heard lots of people tramping around. She asked if we had invited Mr Flamewell. I said he sent his apologies.

I got all the paint arranged and laid out rows of brushes while Sheila prepared food. Then I put pots of paint at strategic points around the house and covered the carpets with sheets of newspaper. Then I rearranged the brushes in order of size.

By eleven o'clock no one had arrived so I thought I had better start myself (although I had hoped I would only have to supervise). I decided to paint the kitchen door. With the first stroke nearly all the hairs came out of the brush. It must have been the one Uncle Walter lent me.

'They don't make brushes like that these days, my boy,' he had said. I hope not. It took twenty minutes to pick all the hairs from the door. After I had finished the kitchen door no one had arrived so I started on the inside of the front door.

When I was halfway down the door, kneeling for the difficult bit around the letter box, it was pushed open violently, thrusting the paintbrush into my face and jamming me against the wall. Askew then forced his way in bellowing, 'Anyone at home?'

On seeing me trying to claw the paintbrush off my face he said, 'Hullo, what are you doing there? That stuff's for painting, not eating, you know.' There are times when Askew can be extremely irritating.

Askew said his friends from the rugby club were coming later. He then prowled about criticising things. I had just finished the front door when Sheila's friends from the Operatic Society arrived. I got some paint and brushes for them but they were babbling away to each other and paid no attention although I hung around coughing pointedly.

Went upstairs and started on the bathroom door, when I was interrupted by a terrible noise in the street, people thumping the front door and shouting, 'Where's the bloody beer, Askew you great nit.' The rugby club had arrived, or rather four of them.

Askew introduced me and I started to tell them what to do when Askew said it was already quarter to one and wouldn't it be better to have a drink at the pub and make a prompt start after lunch.

I started to follow, when Sheila said, 'Where are you going? I am just going to serve lunch.' I said I would persuade them to return. It was rather difficult to prise them away but they came back after half an hour and started into my whisky. Lunch ended at three o'clock by which time the house was covered in bits of food. The Operatic Society were tying paint brushes round their loins like sporrans and doing the Highland Fling.

I suggested they made a start on the painting but they said they had to go off to a rehearsal of *The Student Prince* and thanks for a lovely party. However, I got the rugby club upstairs where I indicated what needed doing. They were the noisiest workers I have ever known. I could hear them shouting and singing as I worked downstairs.

After an hour I went upstairs to see how they were getting on and almost had a seizure. They had painted the entire front bedroom in black and white stripes, like a pedestrian crossing.

The room was supposed to be all white with a black picture rail. They seemed surprised at my anger. 'We thought you'd like it,' they said.

Askew had the decency to apologise. 'They're a magnificent bunch of forwards,' he said, as if that made any difference.

They offered to do the bedroom again but I thought it better to let it dry. We shall just have to live with it. At tea-time Gaye arrived with Hugo and went to do the little bedroom. But half an hour later I found them writhing on the floor together so I stationed them at opposite ends of the house. Hugo muttered all the time. I do not want him for a son-in-law.

It was eight o'clock before we finished. Some of the work is rather slipshod, I'm afraid. Gaye was using a buckled roller which gave a peculiar wavy effect to her sections of

And doing the Highland Fling

the wall. The rugby club painted everything in sight, including the chromium towel rail. But it will do for now and we can improve things after we have moved in. I bought everyone a drink at The Spread Eagle and went home exhausted.

August 24 Central heating men coming tomorrow. They should have come four months ago, before we decorated, but only Flamewell knows why they didn't. This is the last job except for the gas fire and the move. Askew rang to apologise for painting our bedroom in stripes. 'I was a little honked,' he said.

August 25 Met central heating people. Their appearance surprised me, as the advert referred to skilled engineers, etc., etc. There were two of them, aged about sixteen and eighteen. They said they merely prepared the way for the gaffer who would come and do the skilled work. As I had to rush back to work I left the key with Mrs Wainwright so the gaffer can get in.

August 26 Dropped in to see how heating progressing. A scene of desolation greeted me. It was as if Ghengis Khan had passed through. The house was covered in mud and every wall was black with fingerprints.

Going into the garden I saw that they had actually been playing football on the lawn! It now looked as if someone had held a ploughing competition there. They had left the ball in the flower bed. Two spades had been driven in to form a goal. No sign of any central heating.

August 27 Some pipes have appeared among the debris and one or two holes have been knocked in parts of the plaster so I assume the gaffer is now at work. The World Cup is still in full swing, and is now apparently being played on the flower bed as well.

August 28 The men have left and the boiler is installed. At a rough estimate only £30 of damage has been caused.

Mrs Wainwright says 'them two boys' kept kicking their ball over her wall and fetching it.

August 29 I have been so immersed in the new house that I had forgotten we move in a few days' time. Today we started packing one or two things up. It is rather sad as we have been very happy in the flat. It is funny, now we are moving we cannot hear the Australian boys and old Mrs Goldsmith downstairs seems quite nice after all.

August 30 While clearing up Gaye found an old teddy bear. I bought it for her in Shepherd's Bush Market on Christmas Eve nearly twenty years ago. Meat was still rationed. Grew sad and maudlin thinking of human frailty, all be dust soon etc., etc. Eventually forced to take out the Scotch, after which I decided I had a few years left in me.

Sheila and I grew sentimental and got into an argument about when the last tram ran along the Embankment. Gaye can't stand it when we talk about things she doesn't remember and telephoned Hugo for half-an-hour.

September 1 (Poland invaded, 1939): I make it a point of principle never to ask for a day off, but to say, 'I shall not be in tomorrow,' as I feel it lowers one's position to have to ask for a day off.

However, in view of my delicate relations with Sir Phillip I felt I ought to let him know I should not be in the day after tomorrow so I left word with his secretary I was moving house. Young David will look after things. I am rather worried about that lad. He is a charming chap but rather wild and liable to do anything.

September 2 Last night in flat. Went upstairs to say goodbye to the Australian boys and had a drink with them. Of course, they are not the same lot that were here two years ago. As one leaves, another comes. They said I must visit them in Sydney. I said I would love to but I had a feeling I would be unable to afford it for five years. Perhaps Flamewell or Atkins would go instead.

The removal men come at 8.30 tomorrow. I felt depressed but Sheila said we should look forward rather than back. The trouble is that I dare not look ahead for fear of some fresh disaster. I fully expect to find the new house in flames.

After going to bed I got up and looked for the insurance policy but was unable to find it. I am not even sure what I insured and for how much.

September 3 On awaking I realised this is the anniversary of the outbreak of World War II. I hope that is not a bad omen. My first act was to ring Broadwell Street. The 'phone bell sounded, so the house has not burned down. Cannot find insurance policy.

Removal men very prompt. There were three of them. They were called Honky, Bonky and Yonky. At least that is what it sounded like. They did not seem to have individual names but addressed each other by a weird hooting sound. Honky was an elderly dwarf. He walked around with a cigarette dangling from his mouth and carrying toilet rolls and vases. Bonky and Yonky did the heavy work.

I had planned that Sheila and I would direct the operation, but the men took over and paid no attention to what we said, packing first things last and last things first. Some of their methods were rather peculiar. They emptied the food cupboard into the kitchen waste bin which was fortunately empty apart from potato peelings. But it was impossible to talk to them as they were always tottering about with their faces buried in furniture.

We could not find anywhere to put ourselves. As soon as we sat on a chair, they picked it up. You weren't safe even in the bathroom. I went there for a bit of peace and Yonky began rattling the door-handle and shouting, 'Can we have the mirror from in there, guv? No need to get up—just hand it round the door.'

The worst thing, however, was Yonky's comments on our pathetic treasures. His continual criticism became depressing.

'What on earth made you buy this, guv?' he said, looking contemptuously at a large Victorian landscape which Sheila's grandmother left her. 'Know what I'd do with it?

Throw it away and sell the frame. Lot of good wood in that frame. It's too dreary. Casts an air of gloom over the place, if I may say so. What you want is one of them reproductions of that green Burmese woman.'

He condescended to say he liked our Chinese vase, a wedding-gift from my great-aunt who had had it in the family for five generations. 'My wife's got one of those,' he said. 'She got it in Woolworth's on Ealing Broadway. If you're interested in china you ought to look round there sometime.'

When they had almost finished loading there was an odd sort of pause. By a mysterious coincidence all the awkward pieces had been left till last. I had been sitting cross-legged on the floor of the bedroom smoking, and then silence descended and when I went into the living-room they were peering at my books, shaking their heads and making thumbprints on the pages.

Bonky, who was studying an illustration from *The Decameron*, commented, 'Rare collection of dirty books you got here, guv. I'm interested in that line myself. Pity I can't show you some Swedish magazines I got.'

Honky said (holding up Boswell's *Johnson* contemptuously), 'Are you sure you want to take all this lot? They only collect dust. Would you like us to get rid of them for you?'

Besides the books the room contained a few pieces of furniture and our piano. Honky said, 'You know, guv, you've got one or two things that simply aren't worth moving. That there bookcase for instance, and that Joanna. In any case, we shan't get them in the van. It'll mean another journey.'

The piano had been rather a worry. It is very old and Sheila hasn't played it for years. But it used to belong to her grandmother and she remembers crawling under the keyboard on Sunday evenings while the old dear played hymns and we couldn't bear to part with it.

I called to Sheila (who was hiding with Gaye in the kitchen) and we talked it over. Sheila said she didn't mind parting with the piano if it went to someone who would appreciate it. At this Yonky said he knew just the person, an old lady in Hammersmith who'd be tickled pink to have it. This seemed the best solution and they agreed to put the piano in the garden and return for it later for a small consideration.

We caught the bus to Broadwell Street. How I miss the car! But halfway there Sheila remembered she had left her handbag on the draining board so we came back. As we approached the flat we were puzzled to see a column of smoke from the front garden.

It came from our old piano. Honky, Yonky and Bonky had chopped it up with an axe and were burning it. As we watched, they dragged out the metal frame and carried to a scrap merchant who had parked his horse and cart in the road. He already had a full load of bits and pieces which we had been persuaded to leave behind, including the Victorian bookcase.

I went up to the men and said sternly, 'What about the old lady you were going to give the piano to?' Yonky feigned surprise.

'You didn't believe that, did you, guv?' he said. 'It was just a story so as not to hurt your good lady's feelings. I thought we made that clear. You didn't want to take this pianner any more than we did, did you now? We was doing you a *favour*. It's lucky we managed to persuade our friend with the horse and cart to take it away.'

His impudence took my breath away. Unfortunately, as with all rogues and cheats, there was just a grain of truth in his words. However, I was determined they should not benefit and I asked, 'In that case will you please give me the money your friend with the cart has paid for the piano?'

'Money?' said Yonky. 'He didn't pay us no money. We had to pay *him*. Now you mention it, you owe us ten bob.'

I am not quite sure what the symptoms of a stroke are, but I am certain that I came very near to one at that moment.

We arrived at Broadwell Street simultaneously with the gasmen, which was some consolation. For a moment I thought they had come to install the fire, but it turned out they had come to fix the cooker. They said they could not touch the fire, it was another department or something. After about an hour they left, warning us under no circumstances to light the cooker, as they still had a bit to fix.

The removal men arrived after an hour and a half, having, so they said, stopped for lunch on the way, and immediately resumed their criticism of my way of life.

Bonky said, 'These sort of houses are all right if you like old property. If it's not a personal question, what did you pay for this lot, guv?'

I told him and he whistled. 'You bin done,' he commented firmly. 'You could have had one of them new council houses down the road for three quid a week, like I got. And they paint it for you every three years for nothing. The only trouble with a council house, though, is you only get one garage. I've nowhere to put the other car.'

Honky disagreed and thought it was a lovely property, just lovely. It reminded him of his uncle's place in the Fulham Road.

'It's a crying shame it'll have to come down in a year or two,' he added.

I asked him to explain this alarming remark, and he said his cousin at the Town Hall had told him they were going to build a new road through the district in three years' time and pull everything down.

Yonky said he didn't know why anyone wanted to go to the trouble of moving into old slums, he was brought up in a house like this and he'd spent all his life trying to get away from it.

I have never been so glad to see the backs of three men in my life. Sheila said I should not tip them as they have already cheated me over the piano, but I could not stand the look of dumb reproach on their faces and gave them a pound each. As they drove away I noticed all the lace curtains in the road twitching. It was like a snowstorm.

By now we were faint with fatigue and hunger, having been unable to light the gas, but by some miracle the gasmen came back at tea-time, only to discover that the cooker would not fit into the space left for it.

Either the fitted cupboards were too big or else the cooker

was. At any rate we tried the wretched thing everywhere, even in the centre of the kitchen, but it was no use. Wherever it went it blocked the door of the cupboards.

Eventually the cooker finished up in the hall. The gas-fitter said if we liked they would run a pipe to it.

'I mean, that's the modern thing, isn't it?' he said. 'You 'ave this 'ere open plan like. You don't have no separate rooms, you do everything anywhere as you might say.'

I thanked him and said we preferred to cook in the kitchen. They promised to return with a smaller cooker tomorrow.

Noticing a tear in Sheila's eye I told her and Gaye to abandon all further work and took them out for a meal. Afterwards we borrowed Askew's camping stove to make tea and retired late.

Everything seemed strange and out of place. We could never find anything. Even Gaye, who is not the most sensitive of creatures, was disturbed. The house is cold and musty, despite the fact that it is only September, and the central heating seems to work in a peculiar manner. At any rate, the only warm room is the bathroom. Also we do not know how to arrange the chairs in the living-room. There is nothing to sit round, except a gaping hole where the gas fire ought to go.

I wish we had stayed in the flat.

Ten

September 4 I never wish to pass a night like that again. No sooner were we in bed than the night was made hideous by strange creaks and groans and tapping noises. Gaye was so upset that she came into our room to find us tossing and turning. We discovered that every time I turn over in bed there is a creak in her room. Sheila says she is convinced that a cat was trapped under the floorboards.

Fell into a troubled slumber about 3 a.m. and was awoken at five to find the temperature in the house about 98 degrees centigrade. The central heating (which had been put on low to dry the house) had gone berserk. Lay naked on the bed until arising at six to make tea.

It was so hot I padded around without any clothes on until Gaye came out of her room and met me face to face. She said, 'Daddy, you look revolting,' and made mock vomiting noises.

Sheila got up and said the noise of the lavatory flushing is like a mediaeval cavalry charge.

Taking advantage of having to get up early I arrived at the office at half-past eight and left a message for Sir Phillip ostentatiously timed '8.45' but his secretary said he wasn't in today.

Gaye waited in for the gasmen. When I got home they had installed a new cooker in the kitchen. Unfortunately it is one of those baby ones, about 18 inches tall. Apparently it was all they could get at such short notice.

September 5 Rang Town Hall to see if a new road is going to be built through the house but they wouldn't tell me. They suggest I consult my solicitor. I gave a bitter laugh.

September 6 Askew says that when he moved house he had the same pieces of furniture carried through the house and back again in an endless chain in order to impress the neighbours. I need hardly add that he says why didn't I come to him, he knew a firm who would have done it for nothing—no, they would have paid me—etc., etc.

September 7 The 'phone has gone dead. When I tried to ring the GPO from a 'phone box to tell them, it had been vandalised.

September 8 When Sheila went to have a shower today she scalded herself. I could hear her shrieking all over the house. It appears that the water control has been fitted so hot comes before cold and a jet of boiling water comes out before the water cools down.

I wonder what other death-dealing traps lie hidden?

September 9 Was surprised when the 'phone rang in a rather peculiar jangling way about 8 a.m. Answered it and a man said, 'Engineers here, sir, we are working on the line.'

Looked outside and saw they had put up a little tent in the front garden and uncovered the trench. The man who was 'phoning was standing about six feet from me. Tapped on the window and waved to him but he paid no attention and said, 'Can you hear me all right?'

I spoke into the 'phone but it was dead so I went into the garden and tapped him on the shoulder and said, 'Yes, I can hear you.' He became quite angry.

Informed office of my new address. Sir Phillip said,

'Perhaps you will have a little more time to devote to us now.' I do not like the looks he keeps giving me. He regards me with the air of a farmer wondering whether to destroy an old sheepdog.

September 10 Hugo came round. That lad must be on drugs, no one could be so dozey naturally. He says whisky is the opium of the British governing-classes, although why he associates me with the governing-classes I don't know. I did not like to contradict him as he gets so enraged when anyone tries to argue with him, so I contented myself with muttering. Next time I shall show him my union card.

September 11 A terrible dread is seizing me. When I tried to discuss the Christmas number of *The Condenser* Sir Phillip said he would rather leave it until later as *certain changes* were in the air. What shall it profit a man if he moves into a new house and loses his job?

September 12 When I called on the man in braces next door to establish neighbourly relations he hissed 'Cat murderer' and slammed the door in my face.

September 14 Since the night of the holocaust we have had the central heating switched off, but this morning we put it on again as a test. Returned to find the house like a furnace and great pools of water everywhere. It leaks at every joint. Turned it off and put little tins under the leaking pipes. This is what we paid £300 for.

September 15 Rang heating company who said I must have done something wrong. 'It must be your fault,' they said. 'There is no reason for it to leak like that.' However, they will come as soon as they can manage it.

September 16 Am getting a little worried about young David. He asked me if the office was a closed shop today. I said I didn't think the secretaries were in a union. He said he must organise them. I hope Sir Phillip doesn't get to know.

September 17 The central heating men have been and gone. I don't know if they have repaired the heating but they have ruined the house. When I got home this evening (having left the key with Mrs Wainwright) I found they had torn up the wood block floor in the hall and gouged great pieces of plaster out of the walls. The house is in an indescribable condition.

There is a note in the kitchen: WATER TURNED OFF and bits of piping everywhere. We could not find out whether they had finished or not so I turned the water on again and immediately flooded the living-room carpet. I took one look at the chaos and adjourned to an hotel for the night. Gaye is not here as she is working in a coffee bar in Brighton with Hugo.

September 18 But for the expense I would like to live in an hotel. It is so nice to feel that if anything goes wrong you don't have to deal with it. The tap in our room leaked all night and I worried about getting it fixed until Sheila pointed out I didn't have to deal with it.

Went to house early and met central heating men. There were two lads and the gaffer again. I pointed out the damage to the wood block floor and the 'expert' said he couldn't help that, he was a central heating engineer and not a flooring mechanic.

'It's an expert job to replace them blocks,' he said. 'I wouldn't even presume to try.' I asked him about the living-room carpet and he said what did I expect if I had carpets in before the heating?

'You've got to plan these things,' he said. He then produced a form and asked me to sign to say the job was satisfactory. When I refused he said, 'If you don't sign we shan't come again.' I told him nothing would give me greater pleasure. While I could just afford central heating, I could not afford any more central heating engineers.

September 19 Wrote to central heating firm demanding compensation for damage. Sheila says I should not have used the word 'bastard' in a business letter.

September 20 Askew called and fixed his gift nameplate on the gate. It looks lovely but I am rather worried about his choice of name—'The Old Rectory'. Askew says the name will add £100 to the value of the house.

He also says, why didn't we come to him about the central heating, he knows a man etc., etc. I was quite rude.

September 21 Apologised to Askew. It is this wretched moving business. You turn against your friends.

September 22 No reply from central heating firm.

September 24 Have just heard the most terrible news of my assistant, young David. Hawkins, the PRO at the Wolverhampton works, rang up to say that when David was up there yesterday to write an article on the new extension he caused a strike!

Apparently he examined the executive suites very carefully and then told the shop stewards' convenor that the carpet in the room of the sales manager's secretary cost £300.

He gave him other examples of wasteful expenditure together with an imaginative account of his free lunch in the executive dining-room (smoked salmon and hock). As they have just laid off 100 men in an economy drive, the convenor called an immediate walk-out of 3,000 workers.

If Sir Phillip learns the truth, it will be the last straw for me, as well as young David.

September 25 No reply from central heating people. No sign of David. Five thousand now idle at Wolverhampton.

September 27 Ten thousand car workers laid off. No sign of David or Sir Phillip, who is at Wolverhampton. No news of central heating.

September 28 When I went into the old coal shed which is now used as a garden store I found everything covered in water. Flamewell has fixed the lavatory overflow pipe so it runs into the shed. Is there no end to that man's baleful influence?

September 29 Rang Atkins re central heating people. He says I am absolutely in the right and am entitled to substantial damages. He added that I hadn't a cat's chance in hell of ever getting them.

'If I was in their position,' said Atkins, 'I would just sit tight and not answer your letters.'

I told him that was what they were doing and he said hard luck.

September 30 Received bill from Atkins for five guineas. This represents about five shillings per word of his so-called advice. The man is a scoundrel.

October 1 Sir Phillip returned, sent for me, and orders me to dismiss young David at once.

'The staff of *The Condenser* are paid to keep everyone happy, not to foment strikes,' he said. He then added ominously, 'Personally, I believe that if you gave more time to your work and less to your property investments, you would not need an assistant. However, things may well be different soon.'

October 3 David returned looking haggard. He muttered something about having got tied up with a bird in Birmingham. I said, 'David, I'm afraid I have got bad news for you.' He replied, 'You mean they're keeping me on?'

I asked him if he wasn't worried about the sack and he said no, he had already fixed up another job before going to Wolverhampton. We went out to celebrate a happy ending to the affair from his point of view. He is going as assistant PRO to a bicycle firm. Unfortunately, David is completely impervious to alcohol and we continued drinking until three o'clock, having abandoned lunch early on.

On returning to the office David tried to assault every typist in the building (and appeared to succeed with one or two) and was then sick in my wastepaper basket. Soon afterwards he lurched from my office and vanished. Later Sir Phillip came in looking very pale and said David had forced his way into his office and abused him.

'That young man is not to be allowed to set foot on the premises again,' said Sir Phillip.

October 4 The S–Z telephone directory arrived at home today. Only two more needed for a set.

October 5 A man called at the house this evening and asked if I would baptise his child. I asked him what on earth made him think I could do that and he said, 'This is the Rectory, isn't it?'

Really, Askew's wild schemes are too bad. I removed the nameplate at once. I shall *not* baptise the child.

October 6 Letter received from central heating company blaming me for causing the leaks and demanding payment for the repair. I wrote back asking if they would like a pound of my flesh as well.

October 8 Today had the most alarming experience of my life. Hardcastle, the printer, rang me and said did I want them to continue printing the front page of *The Condenser*? I was rather proud of this page, which contained a large photograph of Sir Phillip and an appreciation of his celebrating 25 years with the firm, and I told Hardcastle so.

He merely said, 'You'd better come over. You're in for a shock,' so I took a taxi immediately.

My horror may be imagined when I saw that the photograph of Sir Phillip was still there, but the appreciation had been altered to a diatribe against him.

It ran as follows:

JUBILEE OF AN OLD SEWER

This month our Chairman and Managing Director celebrates 25 years with the firm. These years have been marked by total mismanagement and corruption, and nepotism worthy of Nero himself in the course of which Sir Phillip's half-witted son has been installed as sales director.

Sir Phillip (who entered the engineering industry to avoid war service) has been married for thirty years. His wife is a frequent visitor to the office, where she is known as Piggy. . . .

There was a good deal more in the same strain and a reference to his wife so obscene I will not repeat it.

It was obviously David's last gesture. Hardcastle said he turned up the other day and made some changes just as everyone was going home. Unfortunately the page was re-made by the night staff, so Hardcastle had only just seen the text.

October 9 Spent today hastily repairing the front page of *The Condenser*. The main difficulty is to deal with the 5,000 copies of *The Condenser* which have already been printed. If one reached Sir Phillip's eyes the game would be up.

Hardcastle will pulp most of them but some have already been delivered to the office. I took these home in the evening and to Sheila's surprise staggered into the house and started to burn them. If we burn a few every night we should get rid of them in about six months. Meanwhile the house is overflowing with *Condensers*.

October 10 Received bill from Gas Board, including a quarter's instalment on the gas fire which has not even been delivered yet.

October 11 Sir Phillip complained that the current issue of *The Condenser* is late. I should think so. I personally stole his private copy from his secretary's desk the other evening, tore it into pieces and put it down his own lavatory. Even then I was afraid the damning evidence would turn up in some sewer or other.

It would be just my luck that while Sir Phillip was making a tour of London sewers at the invitation of the GLC the

Meanwhile the house is overflowing with Condensers

front page of *The Condenser* would float past with the insulting article leering at him. I shall know no peace until every copy is destroyed.

Sir Phillip was particularly annoyed over the delay because he wants to send copies to all his cronies, drawing attention to the eulogy of himself on Page One.

'This sort of thing is inexcusable,' he told me. 'You must understand that in future I shall expect you to devote less time to private matters like property speculation in office hours.'

October 12 An ominous event has occurred. Nobby the commissionaire has got hold of an original copy of *The Condenser*. He showed it me this morning. Fortunately he had told no one else. I pledged him to secrecy with wild vows of gratitude, eternal friendship, etc., etc.

Nobby used to be in the Regular Army. How I bitterly regret chivvying him in the past with such remarks as 'All the regular soldiers I knew were too stupid to make a living in Civvy Street.'

October 14 Gave Nobby twenty cigarettes today. Said someone had given me fifty duty-free. But he was not deceived. His face bore a sneer.

October 15 I believe Nobby has shown his copy of the article to Maureen. She gave me a peculiar look this morning and burst out laughing.

October 16 What are the symptoms of persecution complex? I have become convinced that Nobby and Maureen are laughing at me behind my back. And something is brewing up with Sir Phillip. He passed me muttering to himself today. Sheila says it is terrible that things should go wrong just when we were beginning to like the house. I could like it a lot more if the walls weren't papered with £5 notes.

October 17 Asked Nobby what the dole was. It didn't sound much.

October 18 Dug up old flat-iron in garden. Kept it to throw at next door's cat. No sign of gas fire.

October 20 Another L–R 'phone directory arrived today. Unfortunately we already have one. It is the others that are missing.

October 21 The most astonishing event in human history since the Fall of Jericho has taken place. Gaye arrived home unexpected last night with a strange young man called Harry and announced they were engaged! My first thought was that they *had* to get engaged but careful questioning revealed that whatever the cause it is not that. My second feeling was one of immense relief that I shall never have to see Hugo again.

I didn't feel it tactful to mention Hugo's name but Gaye said she realised now what a worthless person he was. She blamed us for not warning her against him. I shall never understand young people or women.

Her new boy friend is comparatively good-looking and his hair is only about eighteen inches long. He is reading Logic. He does not play golf but likes watching cricket if the weather is nice. We must be thankful for small mercies. I peered at him closely for signs of drugs but there appeared to be none. He drinks draught bitter.

We asked if they would like to stay the night but they said they would hitch-hike back overnight as they had to attend a demo in the morning, something in support of some American student leader who has got his just deserts at last.

After they had gone Sheila grew sentimental and talked of during the war when I used to see her to the last tram before sneaking into barracks by the back way. She said Harry reminded her of me. I said my hair was about a foot shorter.

October 22 I will never again refuse to believe in miracles. When I got to the office this morning there was a note on my desk in Sir Phillip's handwriting. I was afraid to open it, as I expected it to be my notice, but after half an hour I got Maureen to open it and read it to me as I dare not do so myself.

It was a personal message from Sir Phillip to senior members of the staff announcing that the firm has been taken over by European Metal Products Ltd! I immediately rushed outside to Nobby, who is the only person with inside information, and he said that Sir Phillip is to be retired with a golden handshake of £20,000. No wonder he had been muttering to himself recently.

After lunch there was even greater news. The new chairman made a personal inspection of the office. He told me he placed the greatest faith in the importance of a lively house magazine and he had been most impressed by *The Condenser* for a long time. He wants me to be editor of a new enlarged publication to cover the whole of the new group! It will be called *The Sprocket*. I shall have more salary and *two* assistants.

Rang Sheila at her office to tell her the news and told her to resign at once, she need never do a part-time job again. She said she had hated the cough-drop factory all the time but had not told me because I had enough worries. She would resign as soon as she had finished typing the letter she was doing.

Just before going home I called in to say goodbye to Sir Phillip. He was drunk. He stared at me glassy-eyed and said I was a very lucky man. For years I had planned a series of insults when we parted but I suddenly found I had forgotten them all so I merely said I hoped he would have a happy retirement.

He said bitterly he would have to tighten his belt, which considering he had just received £20,000 was just about the most stupid remark I have ever heard. After leaving his room I remembered several witty and biting things I could have said.

On the way home I stopped at the off-licence and bought a bottle of wine to have with dinner. Thinking it was the night for fish-stew I bought some Spanish Chablis, but it turned out that Sheila had bought steak and Chablis does not really go with mixed grill. But it did not matter.

Afterwards I rang Jack Askew and he came round with his wife and punished a bottle of Scotch. Askew says why didn't I come to him, he could have told me about European Metal Products years ago, everyone knew they would be taking over, etc., etc. He also offered to adjust my central heating for me. However, I felt so happy I forgave him.

After they had all gone, Sheila and I sat round the gaping hole where the gas fire will go when it is fitted, and Sheila suddenly said, 'Do you know, I *like* this place, dear,' and I said, 'Yes, I like it too. It suddenly seems much better now.'

Sheila said, 'Why don't you give up that old diary of yours, I believe it only makes you more irritable instead of less irritable and you've had enough to contend with over the last two years.'

I replied that I would do so at once when I had written up the day's momentous events. So this is the end of my diary of how I moved house.

December 31 Although I thought I had finished my diary I just felt I had to insert one more entry to finish off the year. I shan't keep a diary next year as Sheila gave me a tiepin instead for Christmas. I am now editor of *The Sprocket* and the new chairman is very pleased with it. I had the foresight to start the first issue with a huge picture of him all over the front page. I personally stood by the presses while it was printed.

My two new assistants are incompetent dullards, so they should do very well in British industry. But I do not have to worry over them as I did over David (who was last reported in Australia). Maureen is still with me. I ask her when she is going to get married but she says why buy a book when you can join a circulating library. I have got her an office to herself so Nobby and she can do the crossword in peace.

Gaye is still engaged by some miracle, and I am trying to persuade them to get married before Harry finds out what she is really like. They plan to marry after taking their finals in June.

We had great fun at the first Christmas in our new house and now we have settled down everyone thinks the new place is splendid. It is so nice to have plenty of room and a place of one's own. Uncle Walter has turned right round and says he always liked the house, it was lucky he pushed me into buying it. Jack Askew says yes, I was lucky to have the help and useful advice of so many friends.

Unfortunately, his friend Charles (the one with dyed hair), who originally persuaded me to buy the house, cannot see it as he is in gaol. He was arrested for a certain offence at Shepherd's Bush.

The only flaw is that despite the coldest winter in living memory, the Gas Board have still not installed the fire. Two men did come but they said they needed some part which is now out of stock. The central heating is still erratic and we need an A–D 'phone directory. But now we are settled these seem mere trivialities.

As I would like to end on a happy note I wish to say that I forgive everyone who has cheated me over the last two years, even the miserable Flamewell. The last I heard of him he was advertising as a specialist in speedy house-conversion.